START WITH

Developing Creativity in Young Children

FITZSIMMONS

Blackwell Education

Contents

The purpose of this book is to show how all children can produce successful artwork. Parents and teachers do not need to be 'experts' to help them achieve this.

Start with art offers a selection of tried and tested art techniques using inexpensive, easily acquired materials and is aimed at all those who are involved with the development of young children.

It is sometimes difficult to avoid imposing adult ideas on children and consequently over-directing their artwork: for this reason I have focussed as much as possible on *techniques* rather than finished pieces of artwork. By teaching techniques we provide children with an artistic repertoire to draw upon. The techniques can be imitated and interpreted and can become something new and unique each time. Many of the ideas suggested in this book involve an element of drawing. I have deliberately excluded a section on drawing techniques because of the many excellent books already available dealing with this area in the depth it requires.

Although this book can be used to dip into for one-off art ideas, we should not ignore the educational potential, in the wider sense, that art has to offer – from the decision-making and organisational skills that take place in preparation for an activity, to developing and extending a particular art theme which is of use in other curriculum areas.

There is no right or wrong way to do art. The ideas here are starting points, all open to individual interpretation.

Try them and succeed!

Overcoming problems

We know that children learn about their world through the direct handling and experience of the materials that surround them. Young children will quite naturally play with, use and re-arrange the materials of their world. When they are provided with paints and crayons, they need no encouragement to use them to create their own visual language which precedes any other form of formal mark-making. Art is a natural beginning from which other skills grow. It is an integral part of the whole learning process, which allows every child, regardless of ability, to communicate feelings, emotions and experiences in a pleasurable and satisfying way.

Whether or not we choose to become art teachers, we are involved with providing art experiences for our children as a natural part of their development. For some of us this poses as many problems as it does for the children, who, as they get older, begin to say 'I'm no good at painting' or 'I can't draw'. Ideas and methods that work for one adult may not work for all of us – the suggestions given in this book may help with some of the more common problems that teachers experience.

'I can't teach art'

Many adults have reservations and doubts about their ability to 'teach' art because they believe they have no art skills themselves. This often stems from personal experiences of having art taught to them as a separate subject at school, at the end of which an exam was taken which was either passed or failed. Adults who feel like this will usually say 'I'm hopeless, I've never been able to draw'. Some of us are very blinkered by our own interpretation of what successful art is, and feel that good art means striving for realism in terms of accurate representation. But remember there are other qualities to explore. How about placing emphasis on colour, texture or design as the major features of a piece of artwork? Try focussing on techniques as a means of developing artwork, the outcome of which is not pre-determined.

It is sometimes an advantage not to be able to visualise the final outcome of a piece of artwork – very often this leads to over-directing children's work and stifling any individual creativity.

Nobody has to be gifted artistically to help children to become creative. We are all capable of developing the skills necessary for successful artwork: skills of observation, concentration and perseverance, decision making, self-discipline, problem solving and confidence building.

Although it is said that children do not need to be taught to draw and paint, what we can do is instruct children in the techniques of drawing and painting from which an individual style can be developed.

'I can never find the time to do art'

Adults who find this a problem very often view art as a separate subject to be squeezed into an already tight timetable. The need for accountability in other areas of skill development puts pressure on us in terms of time allocation, so that the extent to which art is taught will very much depend upon the value we place upon it.

Art offers more than merely being a time filler for children to have a go at once their 'real' work is finished. It should not be viewed as a restful 'treat' saved for afternoons when less concentration is needed after a hard morning's work. It is more than a purely illustrative vehicle for representing factual work. Children can learn a great deal through the processes of arriving at a finished piece of artwork. Recognising this makes it easier to justify time well-spent on creative activities. Why not sometimes use an art idea as a starting point for developing other necessary skills rather than the other way round.

'I can't afford to buy decent materials'

Art suppliers would have us believe that by buying a wonderful range of expensive ready-mixed paints we can improve our children's artwork considerably. Catalogues are full of appealing pieces of equipment and materials that in reality few of us can afford to buy. However, expensive materials do not automatically guarantee better artwork. What is important is knowing how to make the most of whatever materials you do have in stock.

You should make your materials work for you and not against you. For example, powder paints, probably the most-used type of paint in schools, are also the easiest paints to misuse. Many teachers who are trying to economise will mix a batch of paints at the beginning of the week which are far too runny. These paints have to last all week and so they are watered down even more during the week to prolong their life. The result is that the paints are unsatisfying to use and consequently the belief is reinforced that more expensive paints are better. Used appropriately, however, you can achieve almost any effect using powder paints. They also mix very well with other substances (eg glue) to produce different finishes.

It is essential that you are well-organised and set high standards of care and maintenance for your materials. The effort spent on training your pupils to look after the materials and workspace will be more than repaid in terms of minimising lost, wasted and damaged equipment. Avoid offering children too much quantity and variety at once. This can cause wastage if children think there are endless supplies of paper, for example. You should train children to think about and plan what they do where appropriate – you could provide rough offcuts of paper to do this. Encourage perseverance so that pieces of artwork are not abandoned at the slightest 'mistake'.

The art experience is one of thought as well as activity. Allow the children to make their own choices and decisions: the suitability of paper, the size of brush and type of paint used, for example.

'I can't paint'

Very young children rarely need encouragement to paint. They will spontaneously and freely use paint in a totally uninhibited way. Unfortunately, this stage of development passes rapidly for many children and somehow they reach the conclusion that they can't paint. We can help children like this in many ways.

Recognition of the stages of development is vital if we want to avoid making unrealistic demands. It is easy to impose adult standards of realism far too early: we make insensitive comments like 'the arms are too long' or 'the eyes are too big'. While we would hope that a child of ten will be able to comprehend and interpret concepts of size and proportion, for a child during the early stages of development this is unnecessary. First and foremost, children want to produce work that gains a positive response. In trying to do so they may well abandon their natural mode of expression and lose confidence in an attempt to 'get it right'.

We should avoid placing children in a 'failure' situation. This happens sometimes when we have already decided what the outcome of a piece of artwork should be. We begin by showing children a finished piece of work and then show them how they too can achieve it step-by-step. What this really does is to reinforce the idea that there is a 'right' and a 'wrong' way to do art. A pre-determined outcome stifles creativity, lacks individuality and does not cater for a range of ability. What we can do instead is to show children various *techniques* of painting which in turn can be flexible enough to allow for personal interpretation.

Children often feel they can't paint because they attempt to use paints to 'colour in' intricate and detailed drawings. The obvious answer here is to make sure that an appropriately sized brush and suitable paints are being used. We should also encourage children not to make detailed drawings that are later to be filled in with paint. Children often believe this is what painting is all about because of the many commercial painting books which offer exactly this – a bold outline to be carefully coloured in. When children feel they must draw first, suggest that they use a fine brush and 'draw' with the paint itself, or use chalk which defines areas but doesn't become an obstacle. Remember that, as children's manipulative skills develop, we should offer them more sophisticated tools and show them how to use paint in different ways to achieve different effects. This is important if we want to ensure that the child of ten is not still producing the same kind of work as she/he did at the age of five.

'I can't draw'

Children have very definite ideas about what a 'good' drawing is. If their efforts do not match up to adult standards of realism or if they cannot produce a highly stylised cartoon character type of drawing, they label themselves as being no good. But, not all drawings have to be accurate representations of what we see. It can be a very liberating experience to allow children the time to explore the qualities of many different drawing tools – charcoal, pens and pastels as well as pencils – concentrating on what each medium can do. Try focussing on pattern making, texture and colour rather than producing faithful reproductions each time.

Encourage skills in observation and perseverance. It is amazing how many children will sit in front of an object they wish to draw, and complete the drawing without really looking at the object at all. The way we use language is important. By sensitive questioning we can encourage children to think about shape, size and proportion. We can focus their attention on particular aspects of a drawing, without actually doing it for them.

Children should be discouraged from using erasers – these almost encourage a child to 'go wrong'. It is helpful to show children drawings by artists such as Michelangelo so that they can see the many lines that make up a finished drawing. Better still, ask the children to draw in pen so that every mark counts and becomes part of the drawing, whether right or wrong.

'I don't know what to do'

Very often, we leave children to get on with their artwork. We do this because art is an activity that most children enjoy and will want to do with little encouragement. This releases us to concentrate on other areas of skill development during a busy day. Also, we may feel that too much adult intervention will over-influence the final outcome, as children are so open to suggestion.

By continually using art activities in this way, the message to the children will be that we place little value on this area of development. The children in turn will make the minimal effort, may misuse the equipment and will gain little satisfaction from their attempts. If the children are left to their own devices for too long they will become dissatisfied and complain that they 'don't know what to do'. Apart from providing plenty of stimulation to widen our children's visual experiences, we can develop a positive attitude towards art by the value we place upon it ourselves. We all know the value of sharing books with children, so why not sometimes sit and join in an art activity with them?

Allow time for the children to practice and perfect a skill or technique instead of the 'we've already done paper weaving' type of attitude. Allow unbroken stretches of time for art so that children can experience the satisfaction of seeing something completed.

You should draw attention to success, however small. Avoid the sweeping generalisation that something is 'good' to a child who is obviously not happy with his/her work. This is confusing for the child and lacks sincerity. Instead, you should try to pick up on some positive aspects, like 'I like the way you have shaded this area' or 'Your choice of colour is interesting'.

Encourage children to talk about their work and to offer constructive criticism of other's.

Starting points and ideas for stimulating artwork

Working from nature

Children like working with natural things. Make use of local museum services and wildlife facilities. Make collections of natural objects, such as shells, stones, bits of wood, fossils, leaves and flowers in season that the children can use in art sessions. Make use of a school garden, the view from the window, etc. Fruit and vegetables offer good starting points, especially for work on colour mixing and printing.

Machines

Machines are another fascination for children. You could use many types of machines in your art classes, such as old clocks and watches, wheels and cogs, parts of engines, old radios, kitchen implements, cameras, musical instruments, etc.

Famous paintings

These can offer an excellent starting point. Look at the immense variety of painting styles with your pupils. Consider artists like Vincent Van Gogh, Henri Rousseau and Georges Pierre Seurat, for example. Is it possible to visit a gallery or invite a local artist into school? Use museum and lending library services for relevant books.

Visits and other shared experiences

We should continually be trying to widen our children's experiences. Paintings and drawings can be done 'on the spot' and are the most suitable method of recording things that the children have seen. They can then be used back in the classroom to extend and develop ideas. Alternatively, the children could take photographs, from which they can then draw or paint pictures.

Pattern making

The idea of designing and repeating patterns, shapes and symmetry, reflections, spatial concepts and rhythm can all be explored in art classes. Again look to nature and the environment for examples of pattern making – the spirals in shells, the patterns of clouds in the sky, the patterns in brickwork, tiles and buildings, etc.

Colour

You should encourage the children to explore how colours relate to each other by colour mixing or investigating tonal values. The children could look at colours as expression of moods or as symbols. They could also investigate how the effects of colours are manipulated – in advertising, optical illusions, for example.

Texture

Children enjoy handling things with different tactile qualities. Exploring the textural qualities of fabrics, threads and papers, for example, leads naturally to collage work. Think about how you can change the quality of paints by the addition of PVA glue, cellulose paste, sand, washing-up liquid, oats, skimmed milk or anything else that will add texture.

Using backgrounds other than paper

Fabric, wood, walls, stones, clay, plaster, etc can be used for backgrounds. Alternatively, you could change the quality of the paper. For example, you could use damp paper, shiny paper, tissue paper, rough and smooth paper, etc.

Using the medium itself

Use the medium itself as a starting point, for example explore the qualities of watercolour pencils. They can be used with tight control (unlike some paints), they can be soft and smudged, hard and dry for precise lines, they can be delicate, bold or blended. Water can be added before or after to combine the richness of paint with the detail of pencil.

Young children react in much the same way to paint as they do to any other materials made available to them. They have an inborn curiosity and a need to feel, experiment and play with whatever is at hand. The learning process begins with seemingly little help from us, as children find out for themselves about colour, pattern, shape and texture.

In the previous section 'overcoming problems', suggestions were made about how to approach painting as children move on from this early stage of development. We cannot teach children to paint. There is no right way to paint. But we can instruct them in painting techniques which can be experimented with and used in a personal way.

Sugar painting

You will need:

Icing sugar, water, a thick brush, inks or thin paints, straws to use as droppers, paper.

Mix the icing sugar with water to form a syrup-like consistency. Using a thick brush, quickly wash an even layer of the sugar mixture over the paper – smooth, less-absorbent paper works best. Dip the straws into the ink or thin paint and drop blobs onto the paper. Watch the feathery patterns appear. Sugar paintings take a long time to dry.

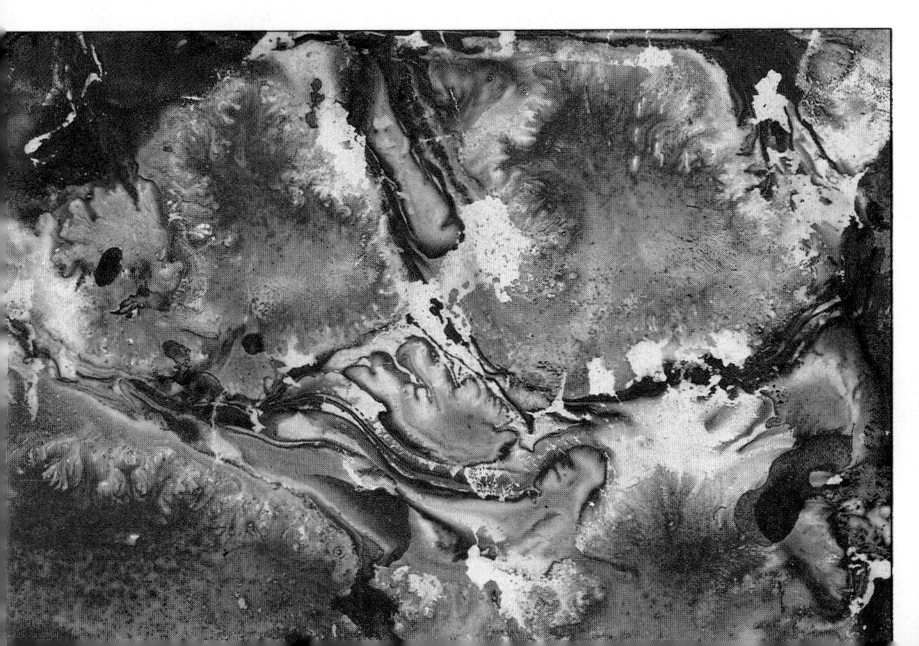

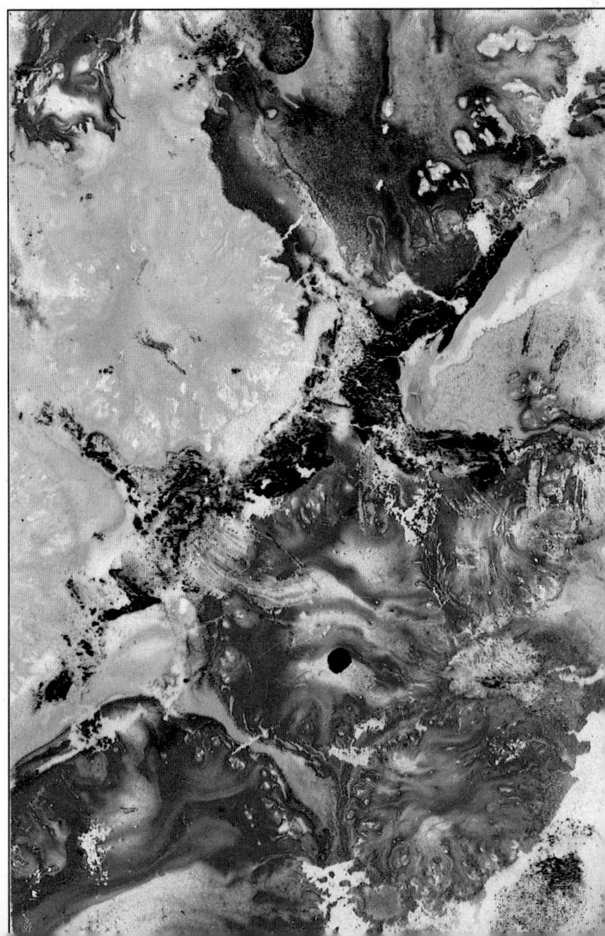

Torn-paper painting

You will need:

Paints, brushes, paper, newspaper.

Tear a piece of newspaper into small pieces. Lay the pieces randomly on some paper. Holding each piece down in turn with your finger, paint outwards from your finger over the edge of the newspaper. Leave the paint to dry. Then tear some more newspaper and repeat the process using a different coloured paint. If you wish to use a third colour, repeat again. Always start with the lightest coloured paint first. When the whole painting is dry remove all the bits of newspaper to reveal an abstract design. Try the same idea using geometric shapes cut out from a newspaper.

Scraped painting

You will need:

Stiff card, paper, thick paints, plates or ink trays.

Pour the thick paints into the ink trays or onto the plates. Dip the edge of a piece of stiff card into the paint and scrape it along your paper. Change the direction each time you pick up a new lot of paint.

Drip painting

You will need:

Paints or inks, straws, paper, crayons.

Dip a straw into a pot of thin paint or ink and then let a drip fall onto a piece of paper. Use the straws to blow the ink across the paper. This will create an abstract design which can then be coloured in. Alternatively, you could add your own lines to make an image.

Finger painting

You will need:

Tubes of ready-mixed poster paint, a smooth formica table top, a board or large ink tray, paper.

Squeeze a little paint onto a smooth surface and spread it out with your hands. (At this stage, hand prints can be made!) Use your finger to draw a picture or pattern in the paint. Now carefully place a piece of paper over the wet paint and press down on the paper with your hands. Carefully peel off the paper. Once the paint is dry, the process can be repeated to add another colour. If you are using more than one colour, use the lighter shade first.

Splatter painting

You will need:

Drawing inks or thinly-mixed paints, a spray diffuser or old toothbrush, paper.

A spray diffuser gives a really even splatter of colour. To use, simply dip the diffuser into the ink and blow. To get a similar effect, you can use an old toothbrush. Dip it into the ink or paint and use your finger to pull back the bristles. As you release the bristles the ink will be splattered on to the paper. The result is a good background texture. Alternatively, cut out some paper shapes and lay them on a piece of paper. Splatter some paint onto the paper. When the paint has dried, remove the shapes to reveal your painting.

Comb painting

You will need:

Thick paints, thick card, scissors, paper.

Paint a background colour or colours on a piece of paper. When it is dry, paint over it with a layer of thick paint of a contrasting colour. Cut a 'comb' from stiff card and use it to scrape a design into the paint. You can also use old matchsticks, lolly sticks or twigs to draw into the paint.

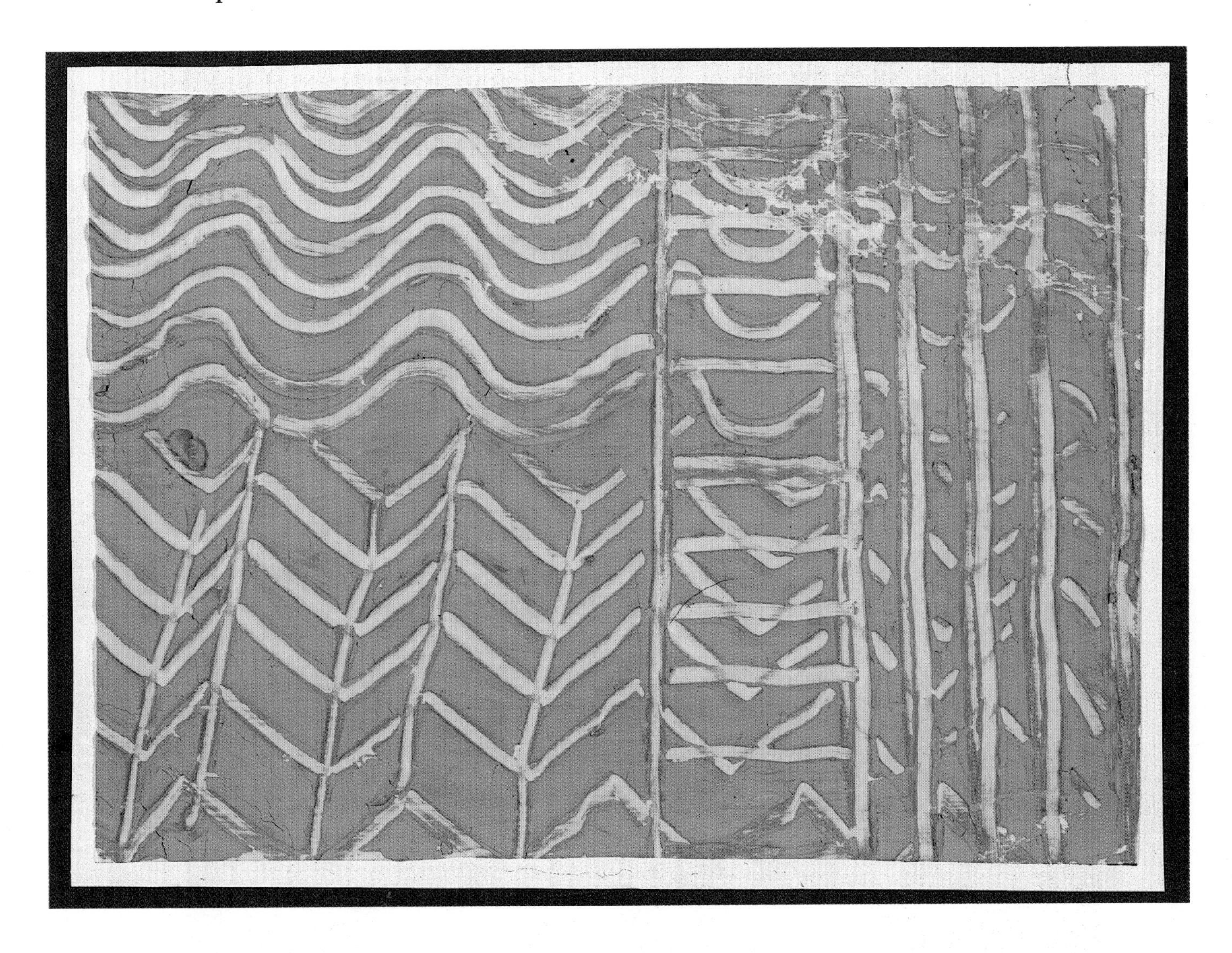

Glue painting

You will need:

Glue that can be trailed easily, paper, **dry** powder paints, an old pepper pot, fixative or hairspray.

Trail the glue over the paper to make a picture or pattern. (You could put the glue into an old washing-up liquid bottle.) Put dry powder paint in an old pepper pot and sprinkle over the glue. Repeat with different colours, if required. Shake off any excess paint. When the glue is dry, spray the picture with fixative or hairspray.

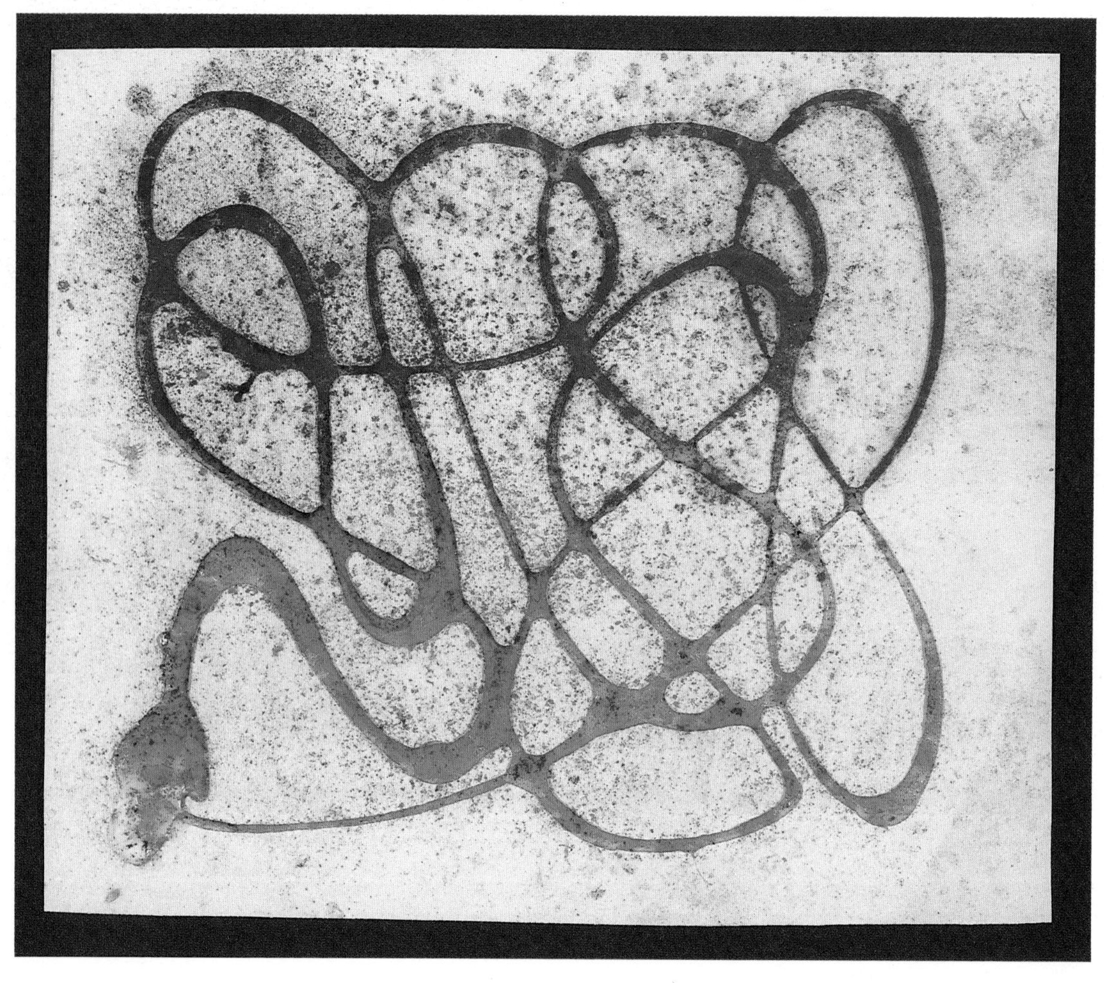

'Marbling' with powder paints

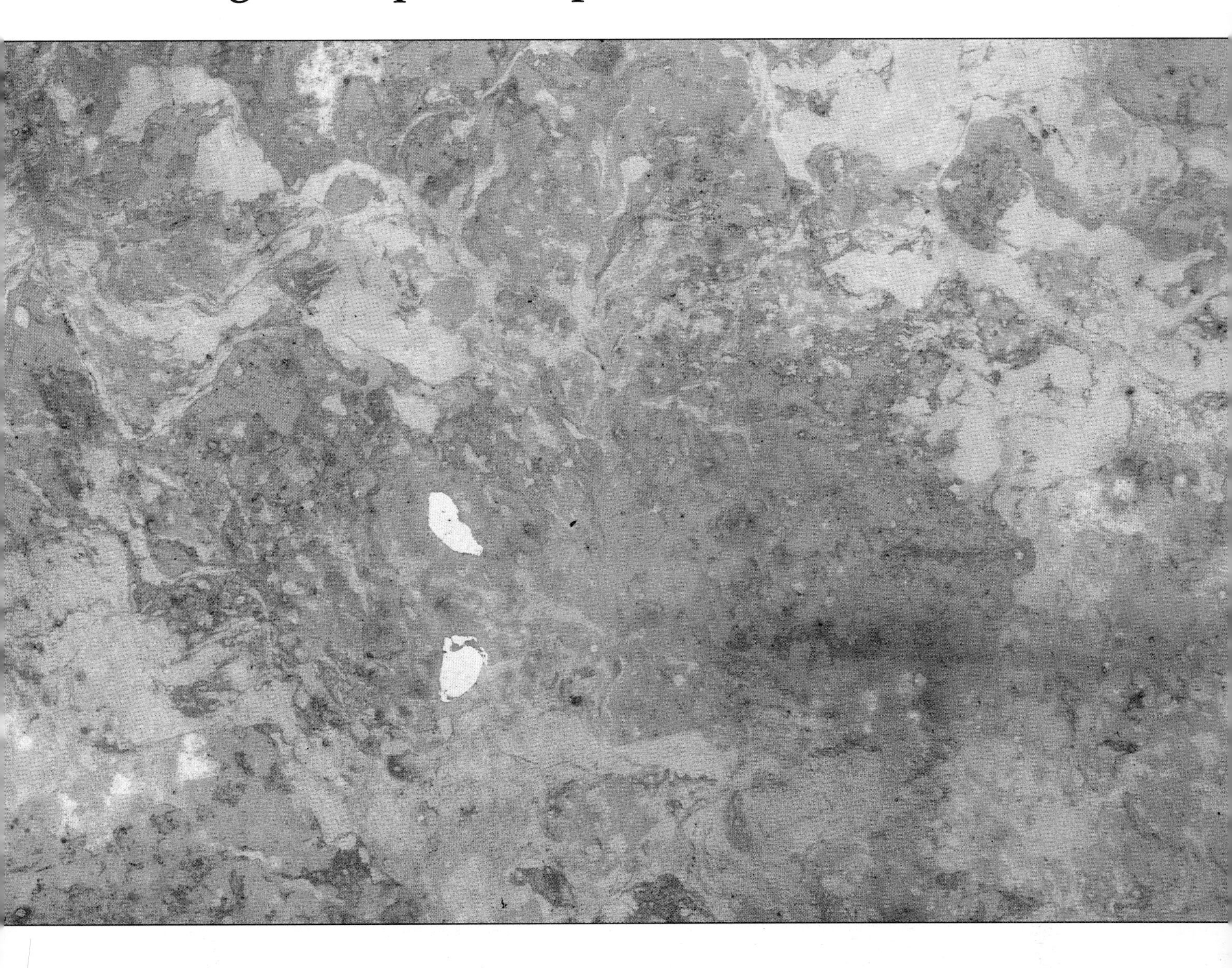

You will need:

Dry powder paints, water in a sink or tray, paper, fixative or hairspray.

Sprinkle dry powder paints onto the surface of the water. Gently lay a piece of paper on the water. Carefully remove it and leave it to dry on a flat surface. This process must be completed fairly rapidly before the powder has time to sink to the bottom of the water. When it is dry, spray it with fixative or hairspray to seal the colour.

Painting on wet paper (stretching paper)

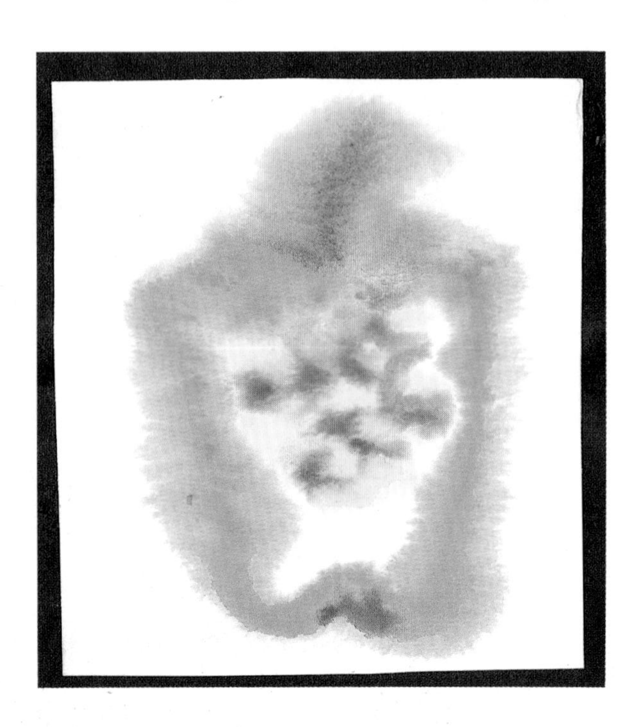

You will need:

Paper, water, brushes, paints, newspaper, masking tape, a board.

Soak a piece of paper in water. Take the paper out of the water and remove the excess water by pressing it between two sheets of newspaper. Then lay the paper onto a board and stick it down along each edge with masking tape. This is a method for stretching the paper and avoiding wrinkles and buckles once it is dry. Now you can paint a picture or pattern on the paper. The paint will naturally spread out on the damp paper to give soft blurred edges. Leave the paint to dry thoroughly before removing the masking tape.

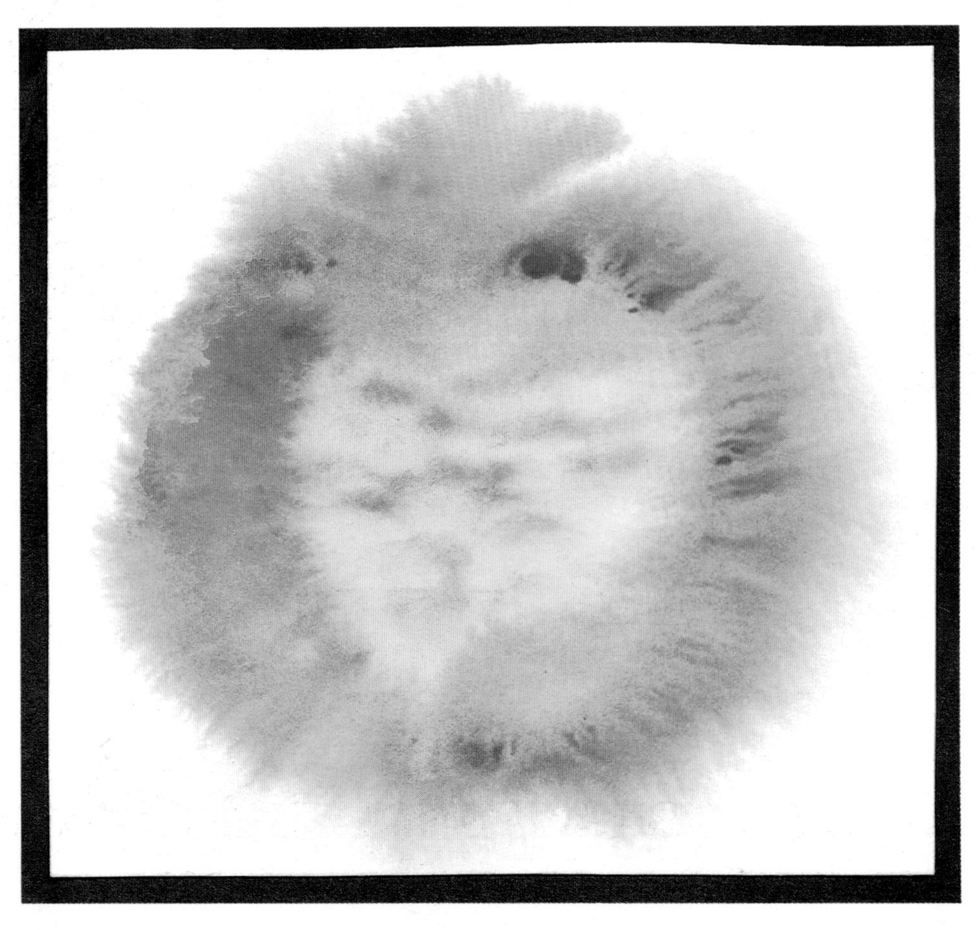

Squash-outs

You will need:

Paper, thick paints, brushes.

Fold a piece of paper in half and then re-open it. On one side of the fold, drop blobs of paint. Alternatively, you could paint a pattern with a brush. Fold the paper again and press it down firmly with your hands. The paint will merge and spread out on both sides of the paper. Once dry, you can add to your design with more paint or felt-tip pens.

Painting on fabric

You will need:

Drawing inks or 'Brusho' dyes, white cotton fabric, needle, thread, beads, brushes.

First, dampen the fabric. Then use paint brushes to paint ink or dye wherever needed. Once the fabric is dry, you can add texture and interest by embroidery or by sewing on beads and sequins. Try adding bits of lace or netting, etc to complete your design.

Combining techniques

You will need:

Paints, paper, pens, pencils.

Sometimes children avoid painting because they find the paint difficult to control and cannot achieve the detail they require. Apart from ensuring that appropriate brushes are being used, we can also suggest that details and finishing touches are added once the painting is dry using pens, pencils, charcoal, etc.

Paper tie-dye

You will need:

Tall containers with lids (coffee jars are ideal), Brusho watercolour dyes, greaseproof paper, string, scissors, newspaper, clothes-peg.

Make up the dyes according to the manufacturer's instructions and store them in tall containers with lids. They will then keep for as long as you need them.

I have tried tie-dying with many different qualities of paper. Thin paper works best, particularly greaseproof because of its strength.

The paper first needs to be folded and pleated. There are many ways of doing this and each produces a very different pattern. Remember not to fold the paper over itself or the colour will not penetrate effectively. Tie the folded paper with string. You will need to pinch the paper together at the tying positions. Once tied, loosen the pleats carefully with your fingers so that the dye will be able to penetrate. Dip half of the tied paper into one jar of watercolour and secure it with a peg. After a few minutes take it out of the jar and remove excess water by dabbing it between sheets of newspaper. Now dip the other half into a second colour and repeat the process. Once the paper is dry, cut off the string and spread out the paper. It will need to be ironed flat.

Examples of children's work

This painting was completed using pens and pencils. Kate Sharkey, age 7.

Embroidery, beads and felt have been used to complete this painting on fabric. Clare Baker, age 9.

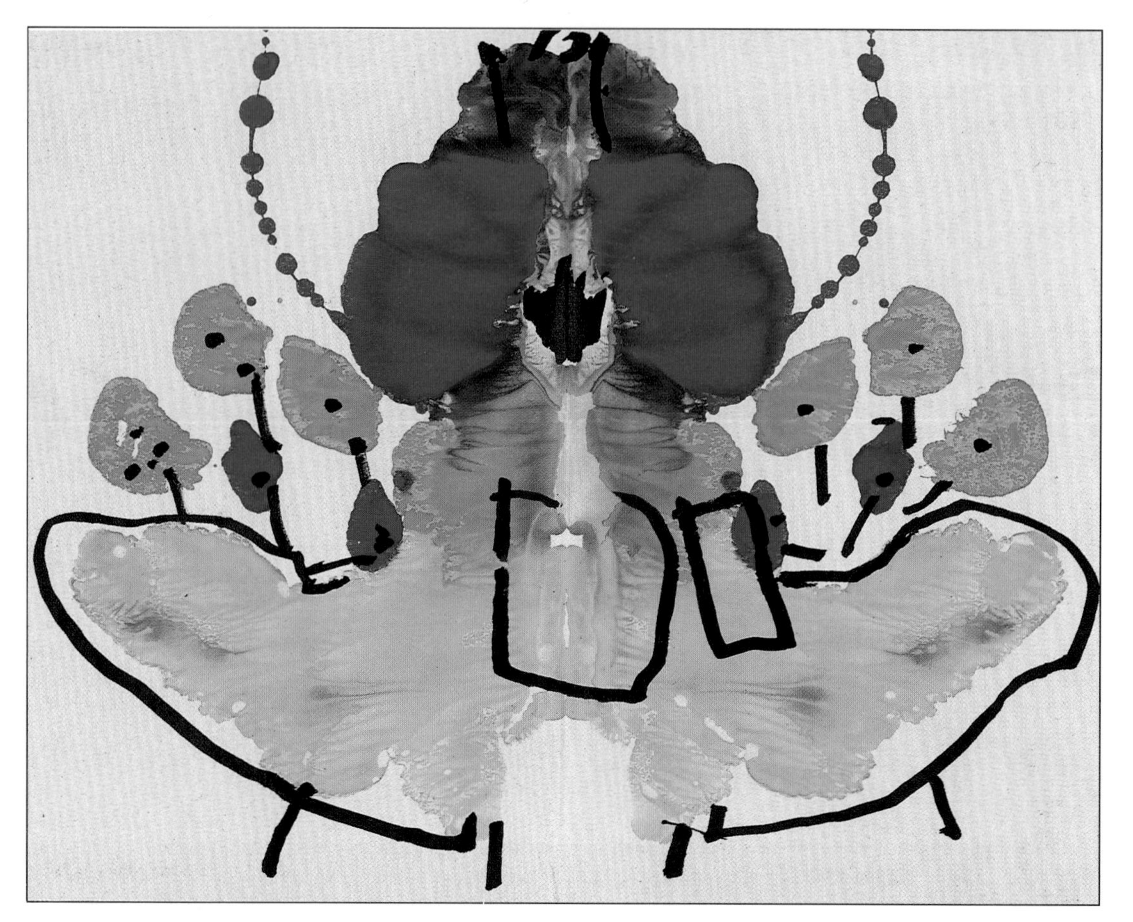

This squash-out painting was turned into a 'biting bug', by Sam Fitzsimmons, age 5.

Finger painting. Jack Fitzsimmons, age 3.

Paper tie-dye. Heather Baker, age 10.

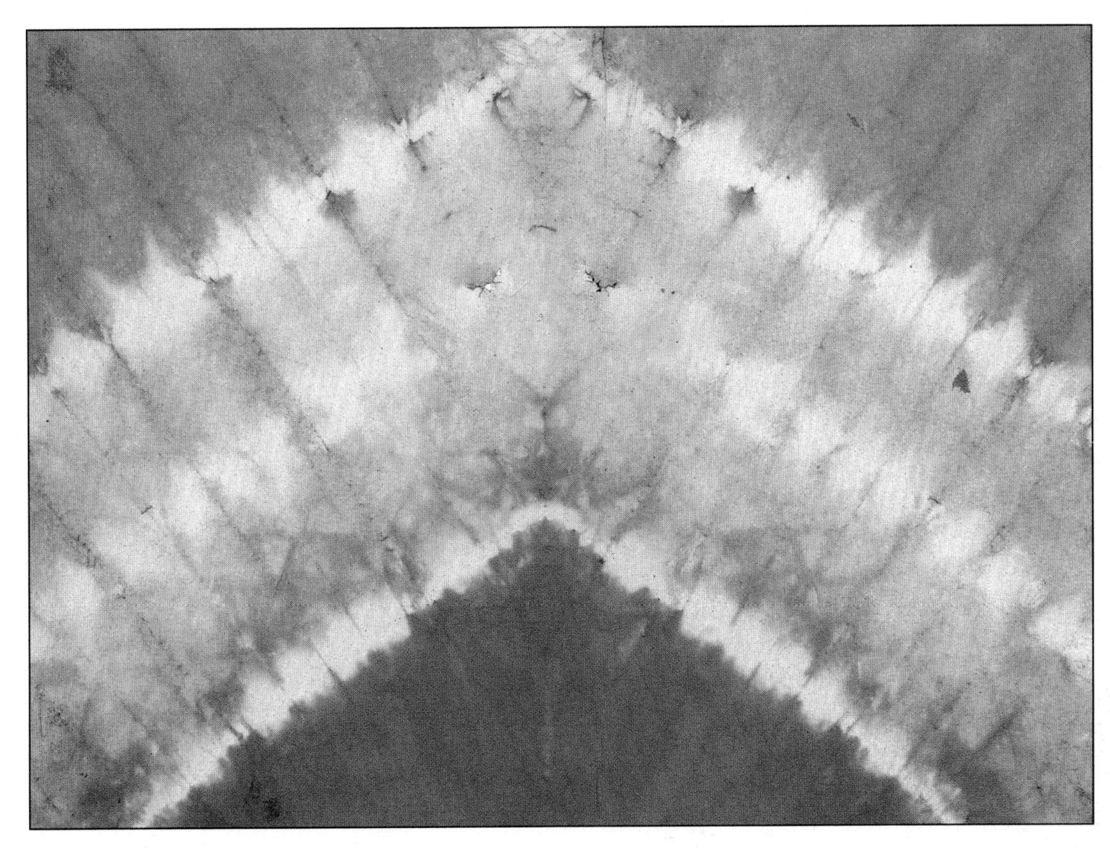

Paper tie-dye. Nicola Lawson, age 10.

Painting is a very exciting experience for children and despite its unpredictability, it is an easy medium to use. All children can achieve a degree of success with paint. We can make this success attainable by ensuring that appropriate paints and brushes are available and by introducing techniques, such as colour mixing, as early as possible.

Once children have progressed from the need to use paint to make their initial exploratory marks and begin to use paint as an expression of their experience, we can think about introducing colour mixing. It is not a skill that should be 'saved' for older children. If we accept that children attempt to make sense of their world through painting, then it seems anathema to restrict them to the ready-mixed bright primary colours when life consists of an immense variety of subtle shades.

This is not to say that we should avoid using ready-mixed paints altogether; there are times when they are appropriate. Any form of paint can be used for colour mixing.

Block paints

Block paints are perfect for introducing colour mixing to young children. They are extremely economical with no wastage at all, they last a long time and are easy to keep clean. Block paints are made with strong dyes so that the colours remain bright even when diluted. Block paints can be used thinly, unlike powder paints which lose their pigment when diluted. Block paints are designed to be used in gradations of texture from thick to thin, and still to retain their depth of colour. They are easy to handle, there is nothing to spill and they offer immediate usable colour. This is important for young children whose priority will be to see what happens when one colour is mixed with another without having to cope with the 'mechanics' of using dry powder paints. Block paints also offer a suitable workable consistency.

Powder paints

If colour mixing is to be attempted successfully and become an on-going development then we need to think about the basic primary colours available. There is more than one shade of each primary colour in powder form; if we can only buy the same shades of red, blue and yellow, then there will be a limited number of shades we will be able to mix. Remember, we want to increase our repertoire of shades to make colour mixing a more satisfying skill.

Powder paints are at their best when used thickly and we should aim to teach children how to mix their own workable consistency. Begin by putting a generous blob of clean water on a palette. Wipe any excess water from the brush and dip it into the dry powder paint. Transfer the powder paint to the palette and mix with the water. Continue to do this until the paint on the palette doesn't drip off when tipped. Remember to clean the brush or change it for another when using the second colour. Train the children to count how many times they dipped their brush into the different colours to create a particular shade. This will be easy for the children as only small quantities of powder are mixed at any one time.

When children master the technique, they will have a vast array of colours available and will become independent in preparing their own paint. Even if the powder paint has already been mixed in pots, it can still be used for colour mixing. This will enable children to find out how colours behave when they are mixed together. If the paint is already mixed, though, the children will have no control over its consistency.

Watercolour

Watercolour paints are transparent and because of this quality, they will mix well either on a palette or on the paper. By simply painting one colour over the top of another a third colour should appear. But the way to really appreciate this type of paint is to apply it 'wet in wet'. This technique creates new shades through the application of the paint to wet paper. It is more difficult to control, but an exciting way to paint.

Whatever type of paint is being used remember that to avoid mixing muddy colours you need to train the children to make frequent water changes, keep their brushes as clean as possible and teach them to use the lighter shade first when mixing two colours. (You would usually need less of the darker shade.)

Colour mixing charts

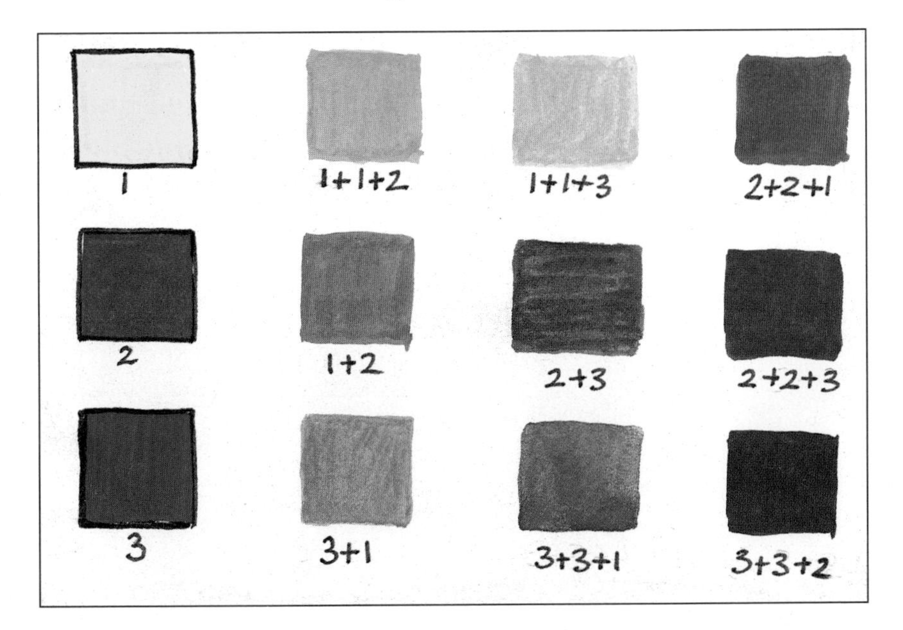

You will need:

Paints, brushes, paper, colour charts (eg from DIY shops).

Begin by looking at the variety of shades available on a DIY paint chart with the children. Encourage them to make their own chart, by showing them that it is possible to create almost any colour from the three primaries. It is a good idea to include the 'formula' above as a reference.

Patchwork quilt

You will need:

Paints – white, black and one primary colour, scissors, PVA glue.

See how many shades of a colour you can mix from the colours provided. Paint a stripe of each colour down a sheet of white paper. Once the paper is full, cut the stripes across the paper to form a series of small rectangles of each shade. These strips can now be rearranged and stuck onto another sheet of paper to create a patchwork effect.

Colour mixing on paper

There are two techniques you can try.

Painting a graduated wash

You will need:

Watercolour paints, water, a large brush, a board and masking tape, good quality white paper.

Ideally you should tape the paper to a board which can be tilted as you do this activity. Load a large brush with plenty of water and your first colour. Paint a band of colour across the top of the paper. Continue working in bands across the paper, each time picking up excess fluid from the previous row. Rather than re-loading your brush with paint as you work down the paper, add more water so that a lightening of tone appears.

Now introduce your second colour and continue the process to the bottom of the paper. New colours should emerge where the colours overlap.

Black ink was blown through a straw on to the dry painting to complete the abstract design shown below.

Painting 'wet in wet'

This technique involves the application of paint to damp paper or to an area already wet with paint. It is a good way to blend colours on paper, and creates feathery soft edges. It is exciting and unpredictable, but plenty of practice will show you how much water to add to achieve the desired effect.

Extending colour

You will need:

Magazine pictures, postcards, birthday cards, PVA glue, paper, scissors, paints or crayons.

Choose some colourful magazine pictures, postcards or birthday cards. Cut a small section from the picture and stick it in the middle of a piece of white paper. Use paints or crayons which match exactly the colours on the picture. Extend the colours to the edge of the paper. In doing so, you will camouflage the original picture.

Complete a picture

You will need:

Magazine pictures, PVA glue, paper, scissors, paint or crayons.

Choose some colourful magazine pictures. Cut sections out of them and keep them as a reference. Stick the cut picture onto a sheet of white paper and use paints or crayons to fill in the sections that have been cut away. Take care to match the colours exactly.

Examples of children's work

Paints and pencils were used to complete and extend this picture. Isabel Hanson, age 9.

Watercolour pencils were used for these extended colour pictures. Natasha Brammer, age 10 (left); Paul Bremner, age 9 (right).

Colour mixing using dry powder paints. Kevin Rowland, age 7 (top); Paul Hart, age 7 (bottom left); Hayley Buck, age 8 (bottom right).

As with painting, young children will begin to find out about making marks with crayons, pens or pencils with little help from us. But knowing what various mediums can do is important if we want children to progress from making their initial exploratory marks. While it is possible that children may find this out for themselves, to fully appreciate what can be achieved, the techniques suggested in this section can be taught and then left open for individual interpretation.

Batik painting

You will need:

Strong paper, wax crayons, a dark colour paint or dye, a stiff brush, an iron, newspaper.

Cover the paper with a thick layer of wax crayon. You could use just one colour or you could draw a pattern. Screw up the paper to crack the wax. Then lay the paper flat and use a stiff brush to paint over the cracked wax. The paint will resist the wax, but be retained in the cracks to create a batik look. When dry, the painting will need to be ironed flat between sheets of newspaper.

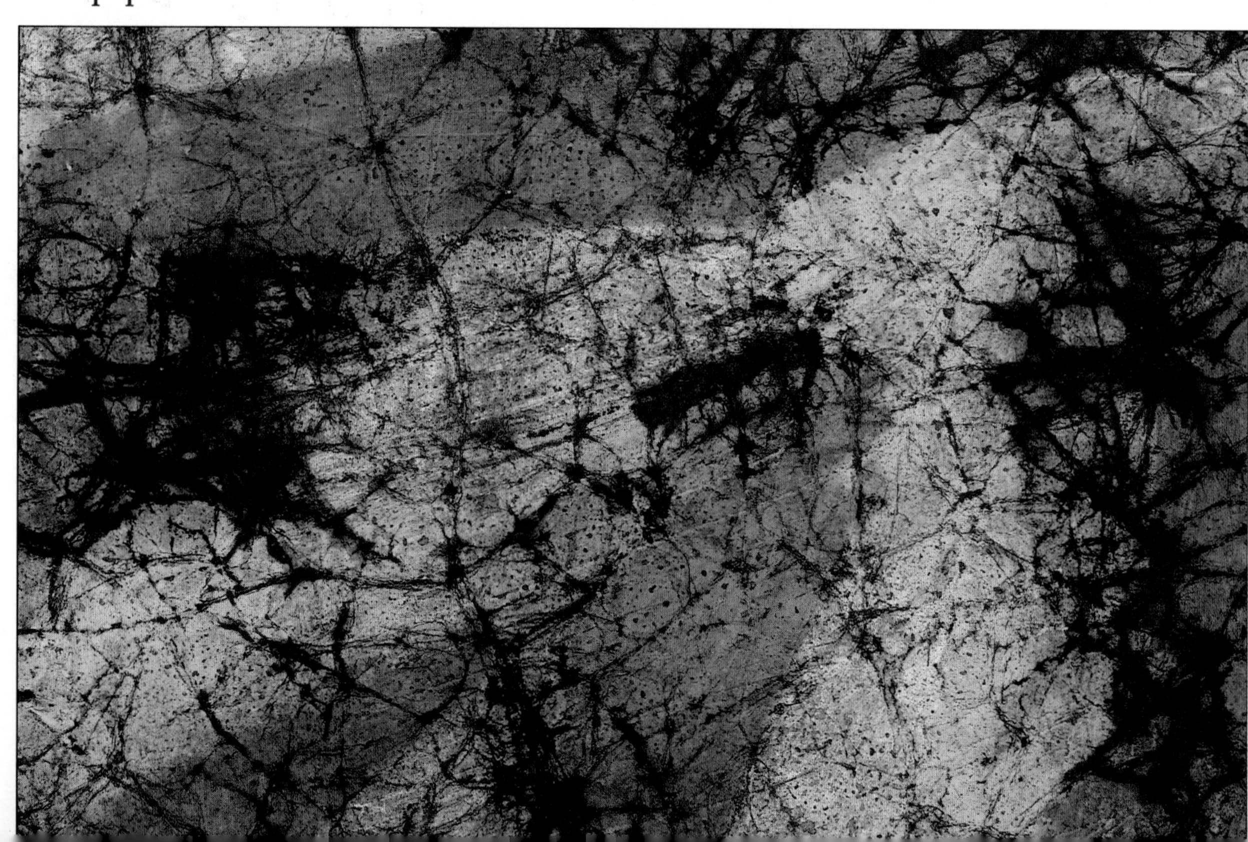

Surprise painting

You will need:

Paper, wax crayons, dry black powder paint, washing-up liquid, scissors or a blunt pencil.

Draw a pattern on a piece of paper using thick layers of wax crayon. The paper should be completely covered. Mix the powder paint with washing-up liquid to get a thick treacle-like consistency. (Mix 1 part paint with 3 parts washing-up liquid.) Then completely cover the wax crayon with a layer of paint. When it is dry, scratch a picture or pattern into the paint using a pair of scissors or a blunt pencil or stick.

Wax crayon mirror image

You will need:

Paper, white chalk, wax crayons, pencil.

Fold a piece of paper in half. Re-open and cover one side with a thick layer of white chalk. *On top* of the chalk, draw a pattern using thick layers of wax crayon. Fold the paper in half again so that the design is on the inside and at the bottom. On the outside use a pencil to draw a design or picture. The areas you fill in with pencil will lift the crayon from one side of the paper to the other to give a mirror image.

Wax resist painting

You will need:

Wax crayons or candles, paper, thin paints or inks, brushes.

Use the crayons or candles to draw a design on a piece of paper. Alternatively, you could take rubbings from an interesting surface (eg a piece of wood). The wax must be applied thickly. Use the brush on its side to sweep a thin wash of paint over the design. The wax image will be revealed.

Chalk and wax resist

You will need:

Chalk (any colour), paper, wax crayons, black dye or ink, a brush.

First draw a design on a piece of paper using a thick layer of chalk. Fill in *all* remaining areas with thick layers of wax crayon. Paint over the design with the dye or ink. The chalk will soak up the ink and the crayon will resist it to give a stained-glass effect.

'Painting' with felt-tip pens

You will need:

Water-soluble felt-tip pens, paper, a brush, water.

Draw a picture on a piece of paper using felt-tip pens. The picture can then be turned into a painting by gently brushing the pen lines with water to make the ink fluid. Do not add too much water or you will flood the picture. This technique is particularly good for producing atmospheric landscapes.

Using watercolour pencils

You will need:

Water-soluble pencils, paper, water, a brush.

Watercolour pencils can be used in various ways:

- as dry pencils
- used dry, but on wet paper
- used dry, then turned into paint by adding water
- used wet by dipping into water first.

These four techniques are shown above.

Children find watercolour pencils easier to use than watercolour paints because they offer tighter control. They can be hard and defined, soft and smudgy, dry or fluid.

Reflected words

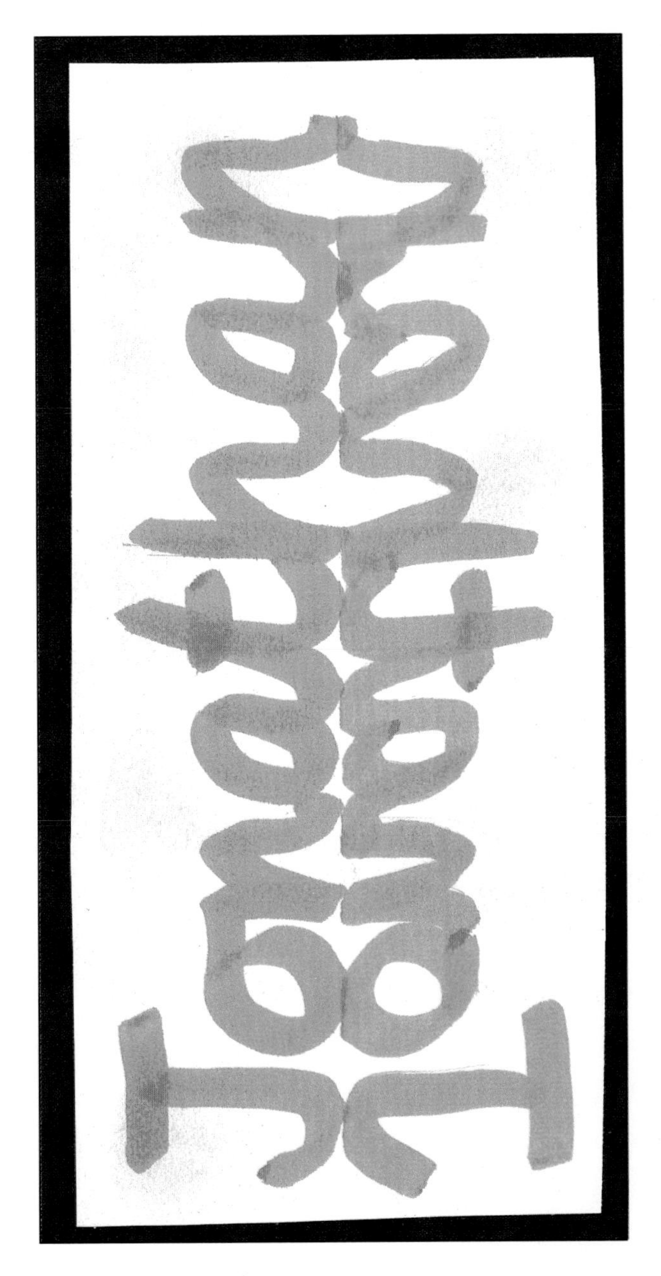

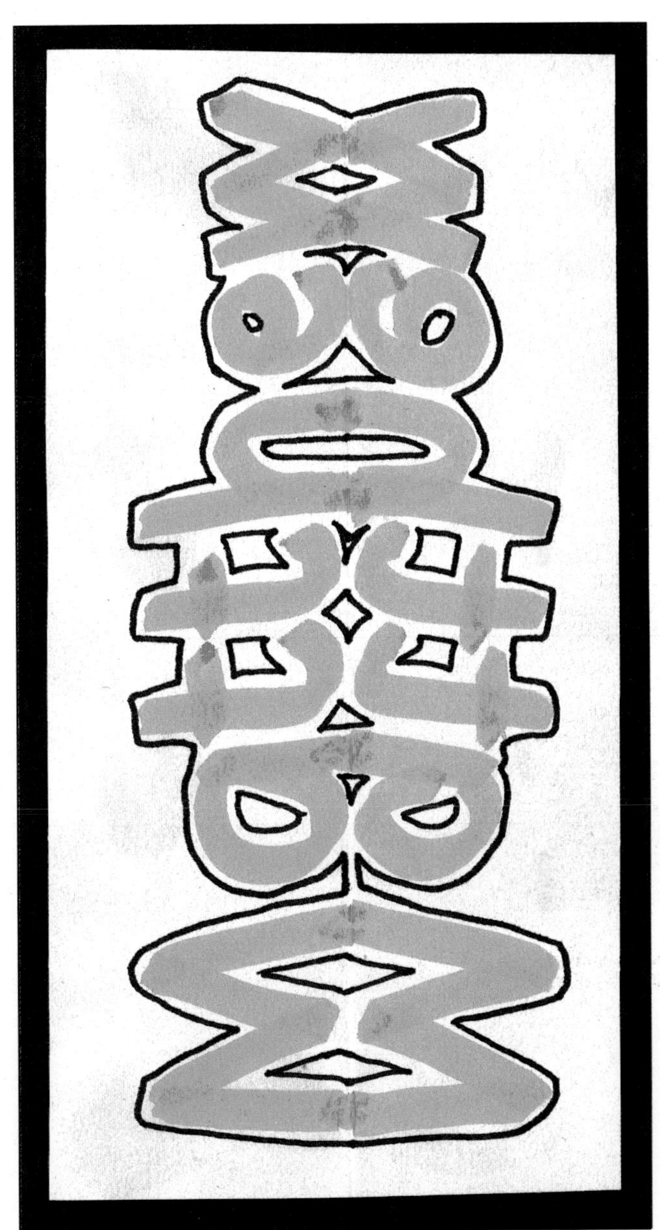

You will need:

Paper, pencils, paints, felt-tip pens.

Fold a piece of paper lengthways. Write a word right next to the folded edge. Turn the paper over and place it against a well-lit window so that you can see the writing through the paper. Trace the word onto the clear side of the paper. Now open it up and turn it on its side to give a totemic design.

Smudged edges

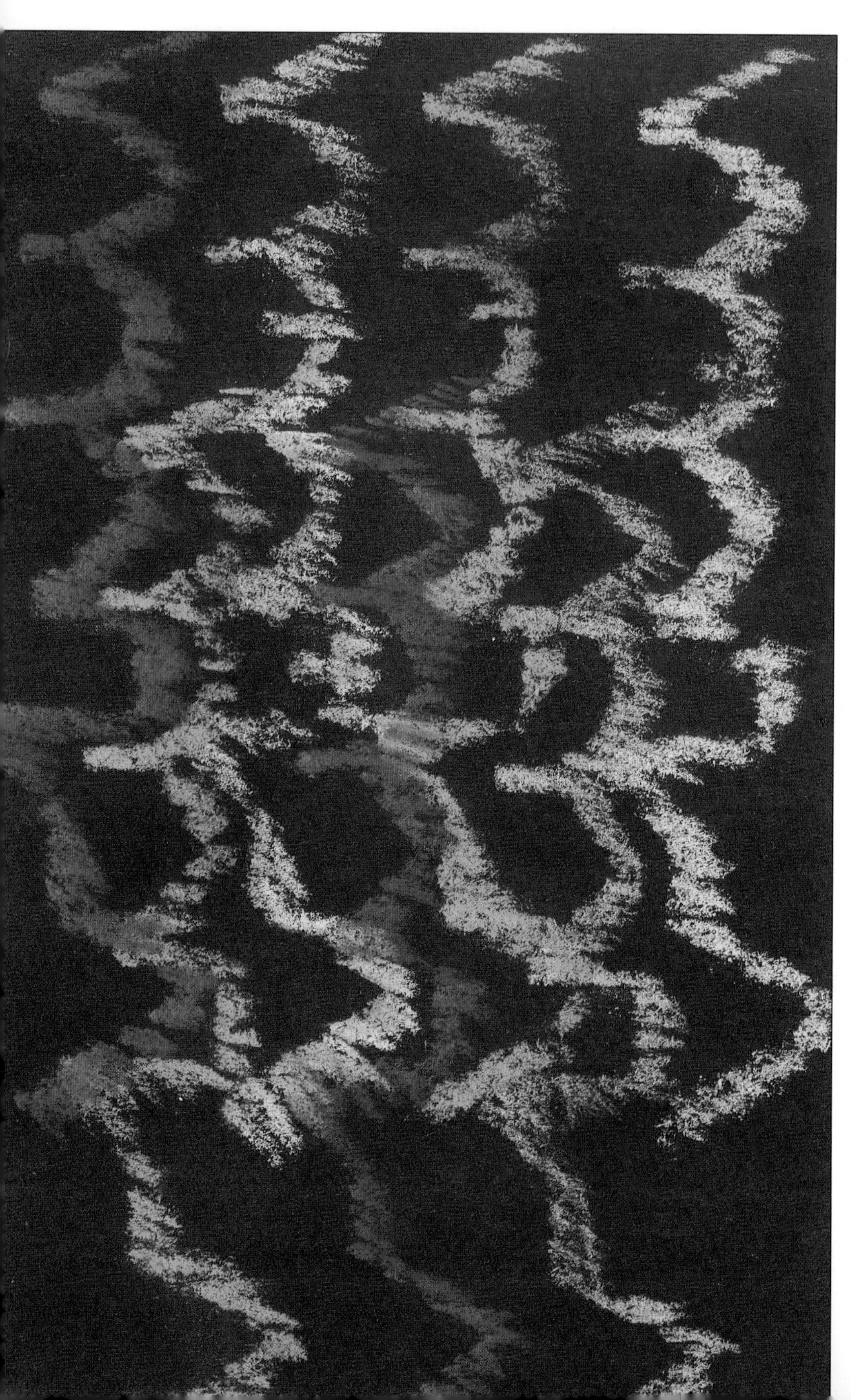

You will need:

Paper, scissors, chalks or pastels, hairspray or fixative.

Using scissors, cut an interesting edge into a strip of firm paper. Lay this edge on a piece of paper. Hold it firmly with one hand and use chalks or pastels to smudge short strokes upwards over the edge and onto the paper. Move your cut edge farther down the paper and repeat with a different coloured chalk or pastel. When the design is complete, fix with hairspray or fixative.

Using charcoal

You will need:

White paper, charcoal, a putty eraser, fixative or hairspray.

Charcoal is equally as good for making tonal drawings as it is for strong linear work. This idea uses both techniques. Using the charcoal on its side, completely cover a piece of white paper. Use your finger to blend and smudge the charcoal to produce an even mid-tone. Then use the putty eraser to lighten some areas. The charcoal can be used to darken areas and to add detail. Some areas can be highlighted by using white chalk. When your design is complete, spray it with fixative or hairspray.

Examples of children's work

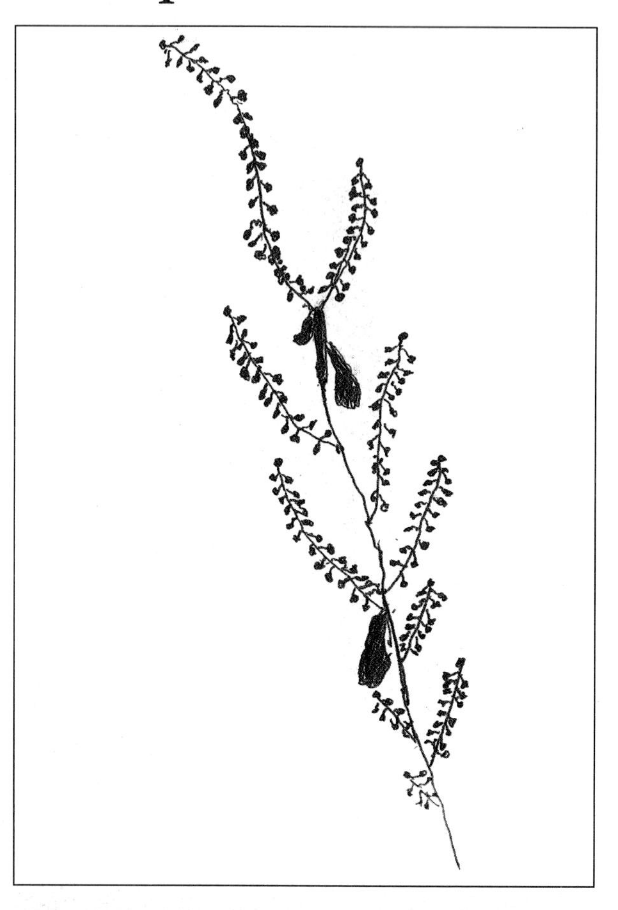

An ink drawing by Nicholas Johnson, age 8.

Inside a tomato. Soft pastels. Paul Hart, age 7.

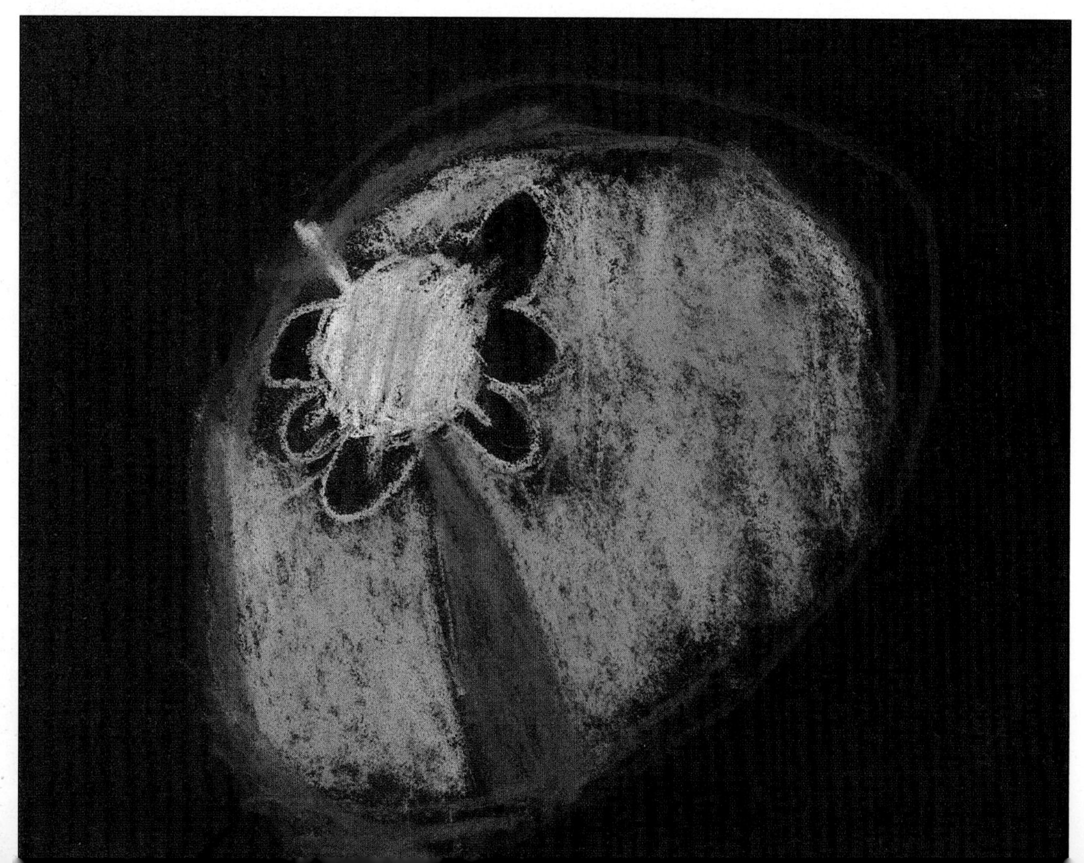

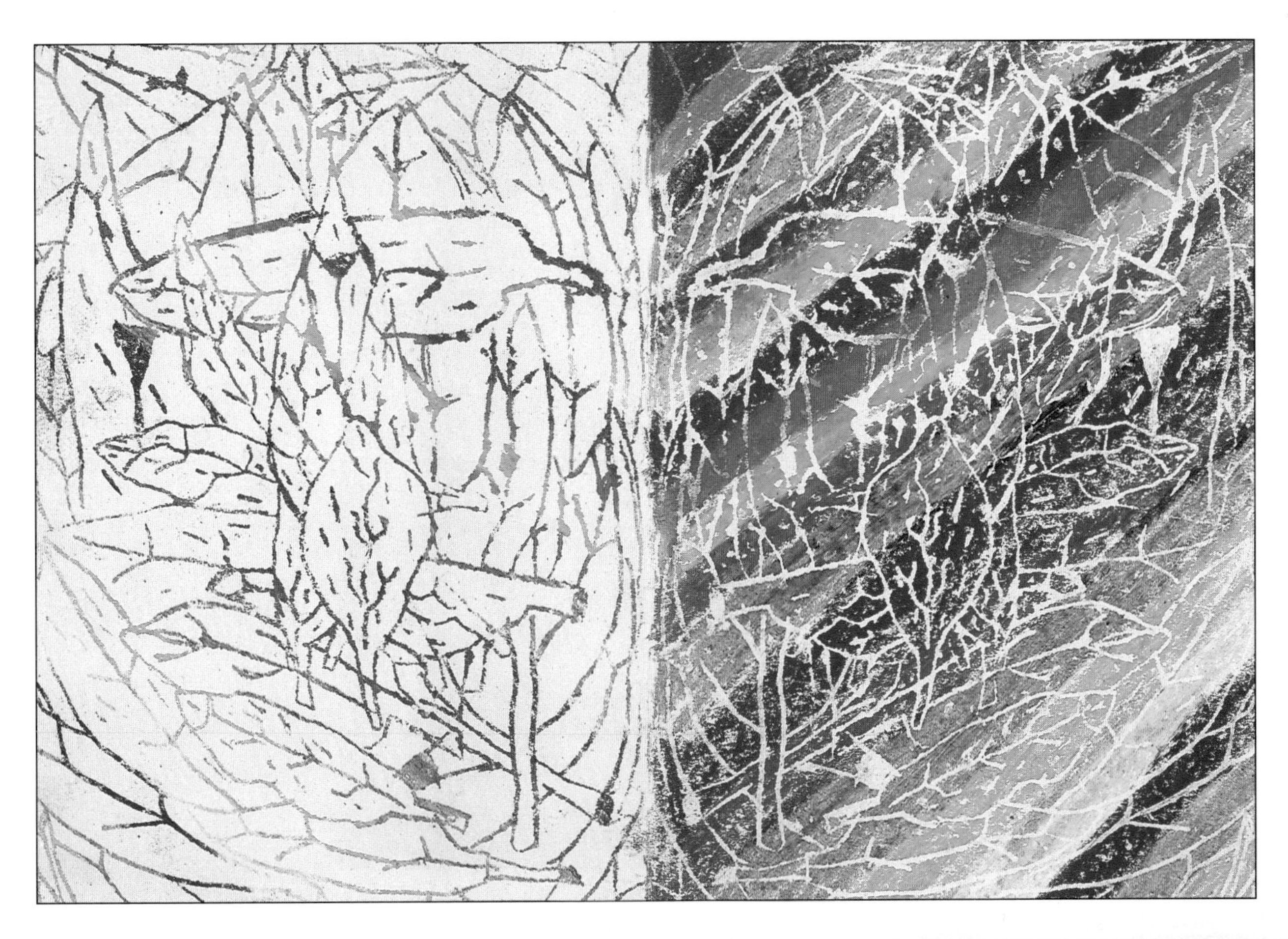

Wax crayon mirror images with an 'Autumn' theme by Lee Butler, age 8 (top) and Markus Rennie, age 8 (bottom).

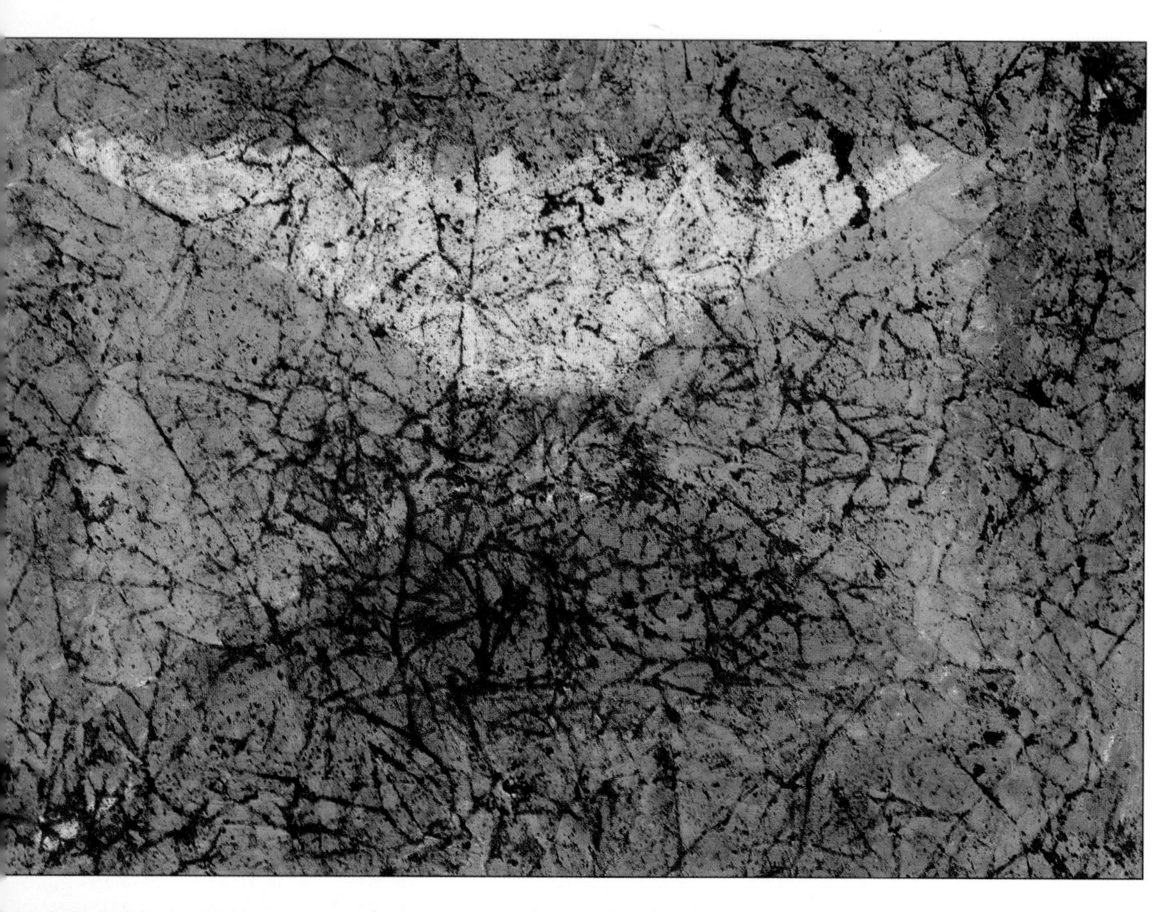

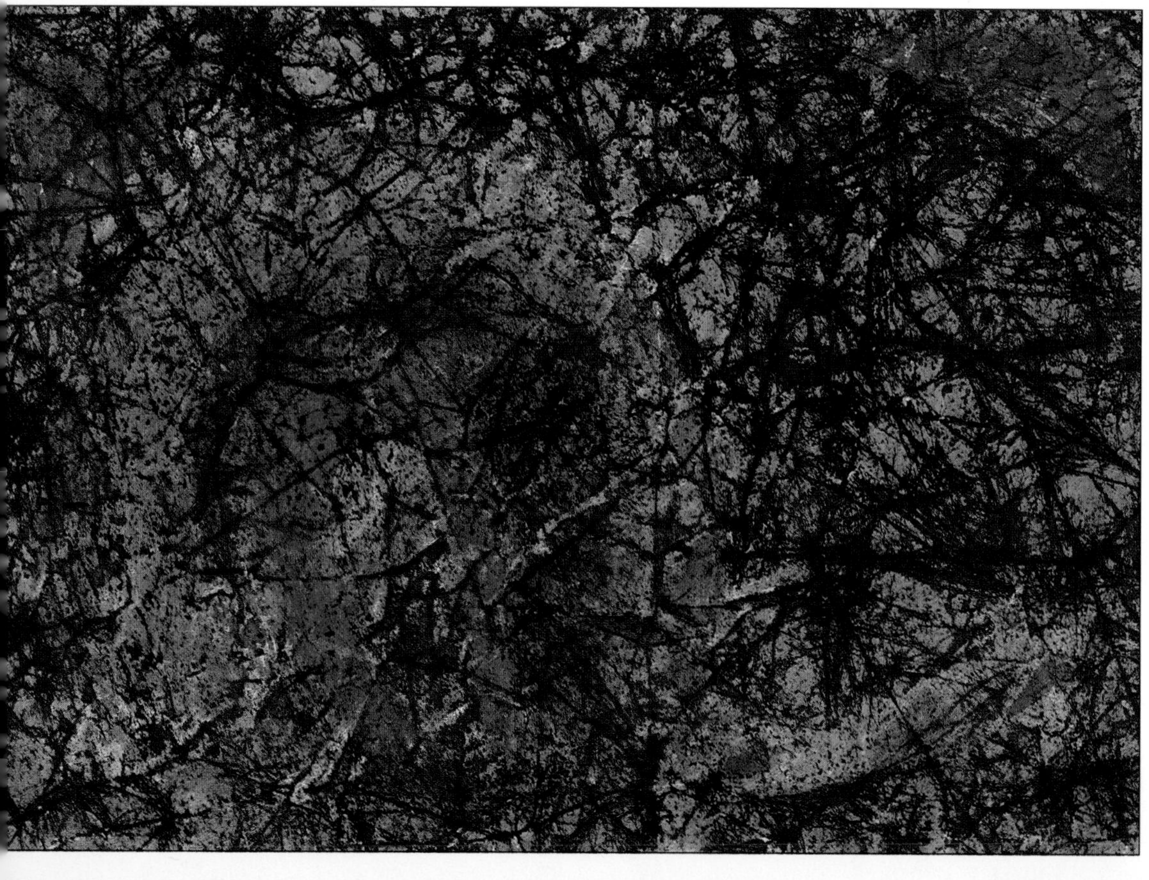

Paper batik designs by Robert Sutcliffe, age 10 (top) and Kirsty Milton, age 9.

It is possible to buy scissors made for small hands which make the cutting of various materials very easy. As with all areas of skill development, the ability to handle scissors will only gradually be built up and therefore should not be saved for older children. The skill should be introduced as early as possible. However, the activities suggested in this section are more structured and should only be attempted after plenty of free experimental use of scissors has taken place.

Paper weaving

You will need:

Strips of coloured paper, background paper, scissors, PVA glue, glue spreader.

Make 'warp threads' by cutting straight or wavy lines into your piece of background paper. Use strips of different-coloured paper as 'weft threads'. Weave these strips in and out of the background paper. Use glue to secure the strips of paper at the back.

Cut and fold

You will need:

Paper in various colours, scissors, PVA glue, a glue spreader, a ruler.

Fold a piece of paper in half. Draw a line parallel to and at a distance from the fold. Draw a number of straight lines an equal distance apart at an angle to the fold. These lines should run from the fold to the line you have drawn parallel to the fold. Cut along the angled lines and then re-open the paper. Fold back every other cut line and stick it down with glue. Place the design on a contrasting piece of paper to complete your picture.

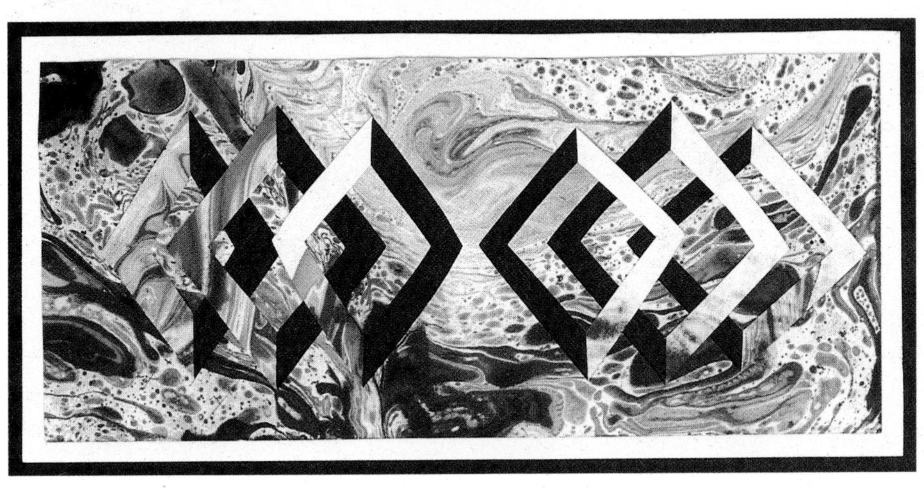

Using pictures

You will need:

Magazine pictures, postcards, photos, scissors, paper, PVA glue, glue spreader.

Coloured pictures can be cut and arranged in various ways. Try cutting and sliding, cutting and spreading out, or cutting and re-arranging the pieces of the picture.

Tesselation

You will need:

Pieces of stiff card, scissors, pencil, crayons or paints, Sellotape, wallpaper or magazine pictures, PVA glue, glue spreader.

Instead of using regular geometric shapes for tesselation, try making your own shapes.

Take a rectangular piece of card and cut a shape from one end. Lift off the cut-out and without turning it, stick it on the opposite end using tape. Now repeat this with the two remaining opposite edges. This shape can now be used as a template to draw around.

Cut out a number of shapes from old wallpaper or magazine pictures. Stick them down next to each other to make a tesselated pattern.

Explode a shape

You will need:

Paper in two different colours, PVA glue, glue spreader, scissors.

Cut a regular, recognisable shape from a piece of one-colour paper. Cut out sections from your shape which can be cut again and spread out away from the original shape. When you are happy with your design, stick it on to a piece of paper of a contrasting colour.

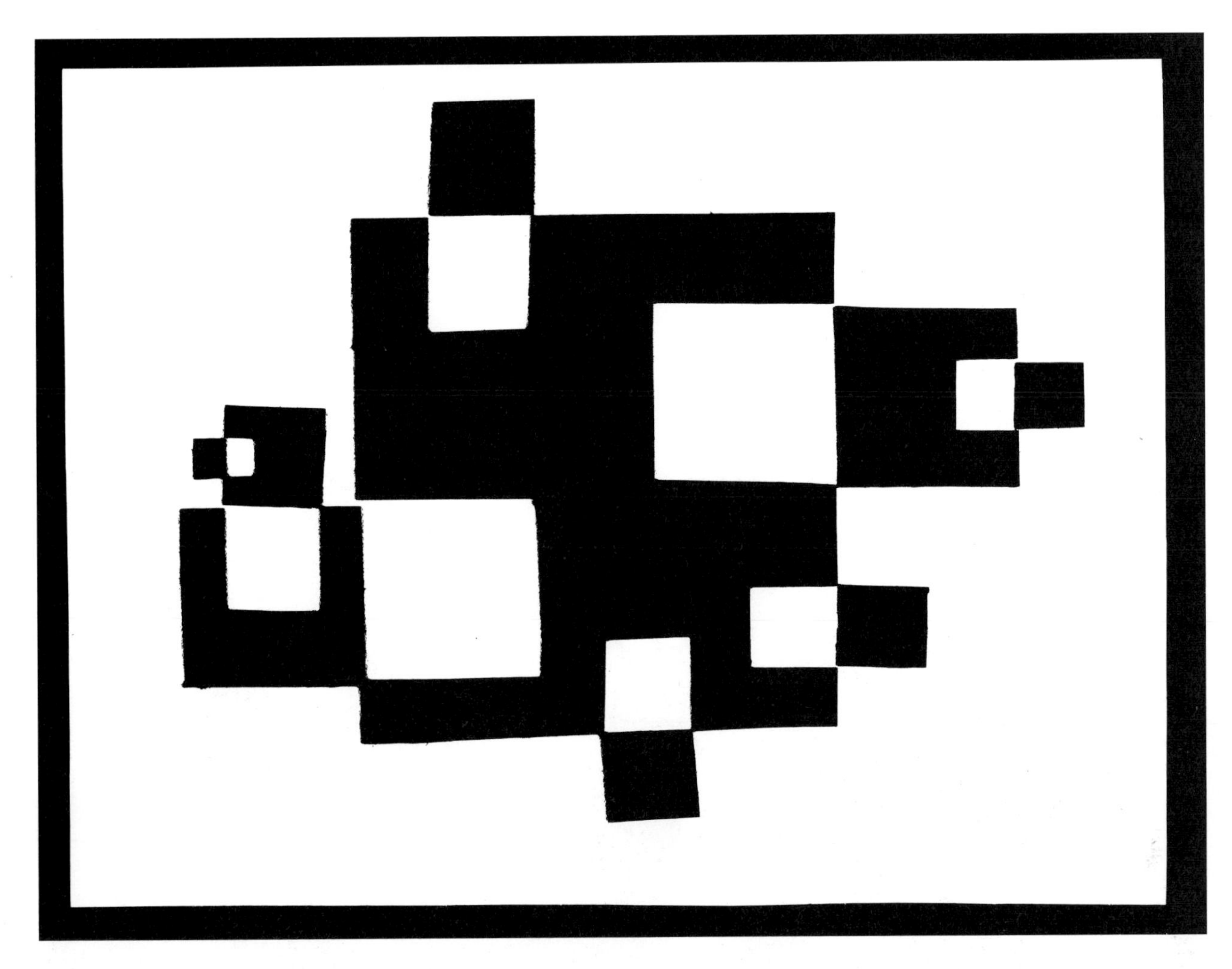

You will need:

Paper in two different colours, PVA glue, glue spreader, scissors.

Cut out a regular shape (eg a square) from a piece of one-colour paper. Cut out smaller similar shapes from this. These can then be opened out like pages from a book. Stick your design on to a piece of paper of a contrasting colour.

Reflected shapes

You will need:

Paper in two different colours, scissors, PVA glue, glue spreader.

One piece of paper should be half the size of the other. (In the picture the black paper is half the size of the white paper.)

From the smaller piece, cut out a number of shapes. Place the smaller piece of paper on one side of the larger piece and turn back the cut-outs. The pieces can then be stuck down to create a positive/negative symmetrical design.

Examples of children's work

These tesselation pictures were designed by Louisa Matthews, age 10 (top) and Luke Griffiths, age 9 (bottom).

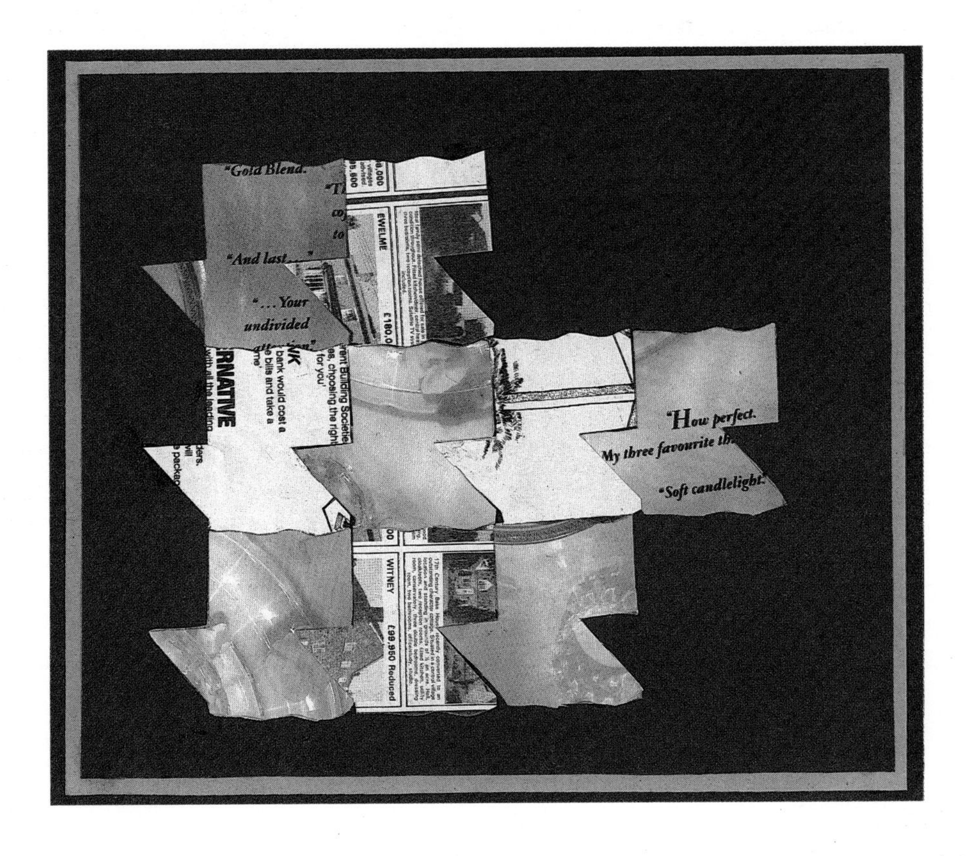

Making collage work

Collage is a method of making pictures and designs by sticking various materials onto a background. Most classrooms will have an assortment of materials that can be used (eg threads, papers, sequins, straws, etc) and most children at some time will have been involved with making a collage.

The provision of an assortment of 'bits' that can be stuck down is not enough if we are to make full use of the learning opportunities that occur when the children are involved with collage work. Left to their own devices children will quite happily cut and stick; many pleasing pieces of artwork appear this way. It is more likely, however, that the finished result will be a disorganised jumble that is confusing to look at.

A successful collage works because there will have been some kind of organisation involved. This ranges from the sorting of materials according to colour, texture, pattern, etc, to the organisation of them onto a background – making contrasts, unifying elements and making decisions about design. We can make these decisions easier for the children by being selective with the materials on offer. Too much choice sometimes leads to confusion and wastage. This is not over-directing what the children do but is instead a more subtle guidance. This is a necessary role for us if we want to allow the children to achieve success.

One of the advantages of using collage is that you can re-arrange your design and make any necessary changes or additions before finalising it by sticking it all down.

Using tissue paper

You will need:

Tissue paper of assorted colours, paper, cellulose paste or PVA glue diluted with water, glue spreader.

Tissue paper collages are very effective because of the translucent quality of the paper. It is possible to create many subtle shades by overlapping different colours of paper. Cutting and tearing the paper will give quite different results as well.

Using natural objects

You will need:

Leaves, pressed flowers, seeds, grasses, twigs, berries, pieces of bark, feathers, and any other natural objects, PVA glue diluted with water, strong paper or card, brush.

Collect any natural objects that can be arranged and stuck onto a strong paper or card background. To make your collage last longer you can seal it with a layer of PVA glue diluted with water. This will dry to a transparent glossy finish. Wash the brush immediately to remove all traces of glue.

Using various papers

You will need:

An assortment of different papers (eg newspaper, shiny paper, tissue paper, sugar paper), cellulose paste or PVA glue diluted with water, glue spreader, background paper.

Paper collages do not have to be flat. It is easy to achieve a three-dimensional sculptured look. Experiment with different types of paper by tearing, cutting, scrunching, pleating, folding, etc. You can then make a pattern or picture from any of these assorted papers. The collage below was made by cutting out a number of identical shapes from different sorts of paper and sticking them down in a regular pattern.

Using dried food

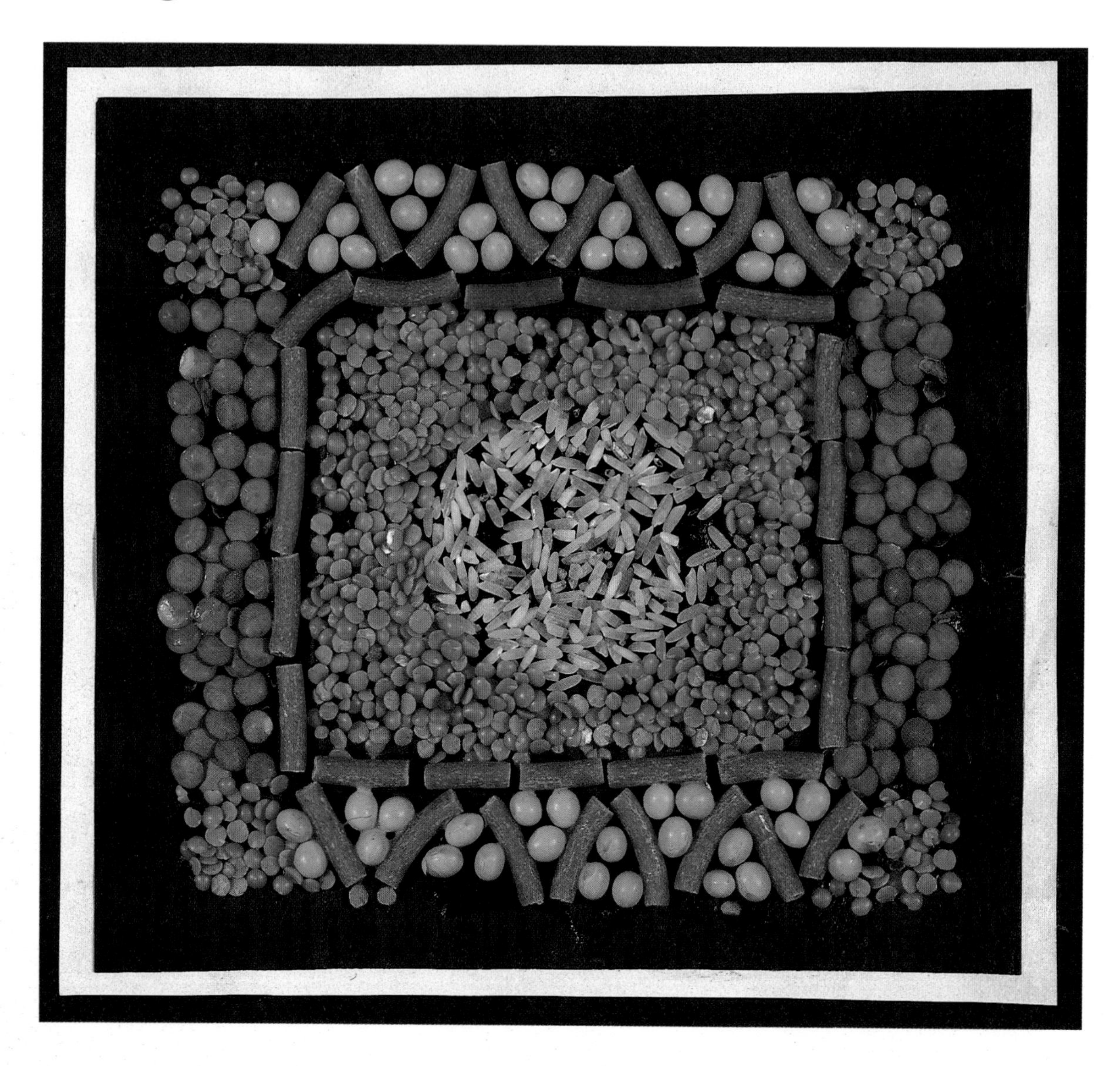

You will need:

Pasta shapes, rice, lentils, peas, beans, bits of egg shell, sea salt, PVA glue, glue spreader, paints and brushes, strong paper or card.

This type of collage works best if you make full use of the contrasting colours, shapes and textures you have available. It is much easier to apply the glue to the background and stick bits on rather than trying to glue each separate piece. You can also create your own colour schemes by painting pieces *before* you stick them on to the paper.

Using fabrics and threads

You will need:

An assortment of fabrics, threads, string and netting, PVA glue, glue spreader, strong background paper or card.

As with most collages, using fabrics and threads will be successful if some thought is given to how the materials work together. For example, contrast colours, textures and patterns or try focussing on shades of a particular colour to create a successful effect.

Egg-shell mosaics

You will need:

Clean egg-shells, paper, paint, PVA glue, glue spreader, trays to put egg-shells in.

Paint the shells and leave them until they are thoroughly dry. It is easier to keep different-coloured egg-shells in separate trays. Draw a design or outline on a piece of paper. Break off large pieces of egg-shell. Apply glue to the design and then press the egg shell firmly down with your finger, breaking it at the same time.

Alternatively, the egg-shells can be stuck down and then painted. You will need a steady hand for this, though.

Egg-shells also look effective as decorations for small trinket boxes or photo frames.

Examples of children's work

Two types of paper were used to make this collage.

Matthew Drew, age 4.

Wax crayon rubbings were taken from a card printing block. A wash of thin paint was then added. Fabric, thread and tissue paper were used to complete this underwater picture. Kevin Rowland, age 7.

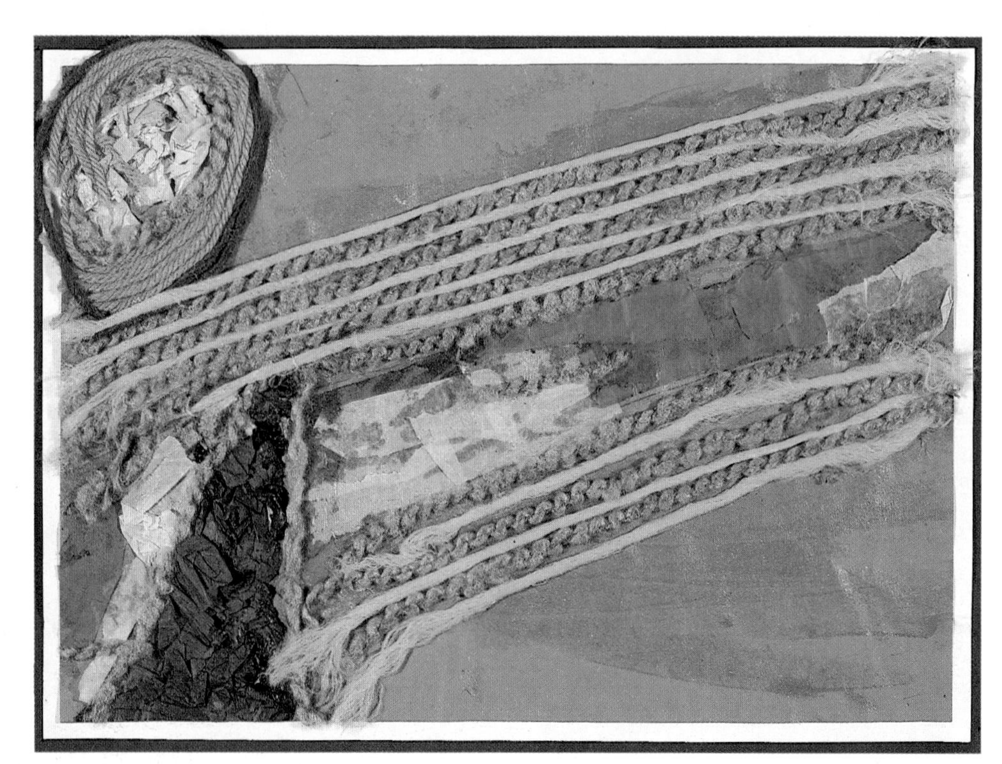

These three collages were completed after looking at Vincent Van Gogh's 'Starry Night'. The children used tissue paper and assorted threads. Gillian Colley, age 9 (top); Melanie Thurgood, age 8 (bottom left); Michael Harvey, age 9 (bottom right).

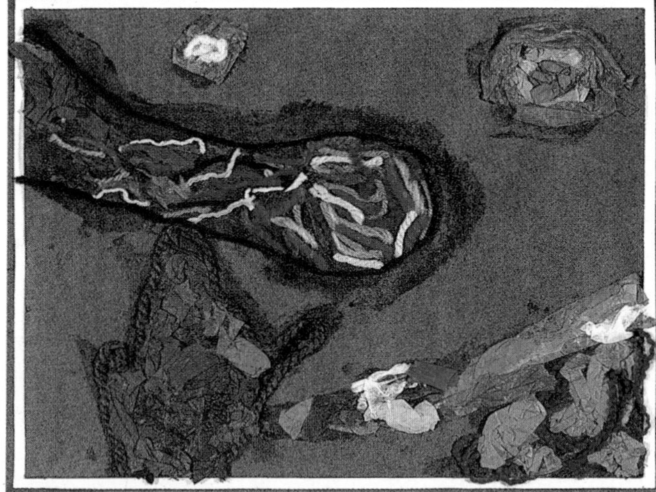

Printing

Anything with an interesting surface texture can be used to print with. For example, leaves, fabric, vegetables, Lego, cotton reels, corks, etc. You can also make your own printing blocks by sticking string, card, sponge, etc, onto a thick card base.

Printing blocks can be inked using either rollers or brushes and printing inks or paints. An ink pad can also be used to ink objects. You can make an ink pad with a sponge or felt soaked in ink or paint kept in a saucer.

To get this effect, a leaf was painted and a sheet of paper placed on top. This was then gently rolled over with a clean roller. The paper was then lifted off to reveal the leaf pattern.

Printing with card

You will need:

Stiff card, corrugated card, printing ink, ink tray, rollers, scissors, PVA glue, newspaper and paper.

Cut a design from card or corrugated card and stick it onto a card base board to make a printing block. Seal the surface of the printing block by covering it with a layer of glue. This will prolong its life. Use a roller to ink up the block. Lay the inked block face down on a piece of paper. Cover it with a sheet of newspaper and roll over it firmly with a clean roller. Remove the newspaper and printing block to reveal an image which can then be repeated to build up a design.

Printing with polyblocks

You will need:

Polyblocks, a blunt pencil, printing inks and trays, roller, newspaper, paper.

Polyblocks are thin polystyrene tiles which can be used to produce simple line images or more sophisticated designs using several colours.

Score a line drawing on the block using a blunt pencil. Then use a roller to ink up the block. Lay the inked block face down on a piece of paper. Cover it with a sheet of newspaper and firmly roll over it with a clean roller. You will then have a print of the area not drawn on with the pencil.

If more than one colour is to be used, then start as above by scoring a pattern into your polyblock. Ink up the block with your first colour and print. Before you print your second colour, you should block out some other areas using your blunt pencil. This process should be repeated for each new colour. In the picture below, the outline of a leaf was first scored into the polyblock and a print was made with yellow ink. Parts of the leaf were then blocked out and a print was made with green ink. Finally, all the area within the leaf was scored out with the pencil and a print was made with brown ink.

Remember these points:

- always use the lightest colour first
- place your paper on a wad of newspaper before you use your printing block – this will give you a more receptive surface than a hard table
- mark around each corner of the block with a pencil the first time you print. You can then line up your block exactly when you use a different colour, so that the image stays in line.

Repeat patterns

You will need:

Printing blocks made from card, potato, Plasticine, lino cuts, polyblocks, etc, paint or printing ink, paper, brushes or rollers, ink trays.

Explore the idea of pattern making and design by using regularly shaped printing blocks. Once you have made your printing block, mark a notch at the top of it. Make a pattern by rotating your block through 90° after each print. You can keep track of where you are by watching where the notch on your block is each time you make a print. You can now design your own tiles or print your own fabric or wrapping paper.

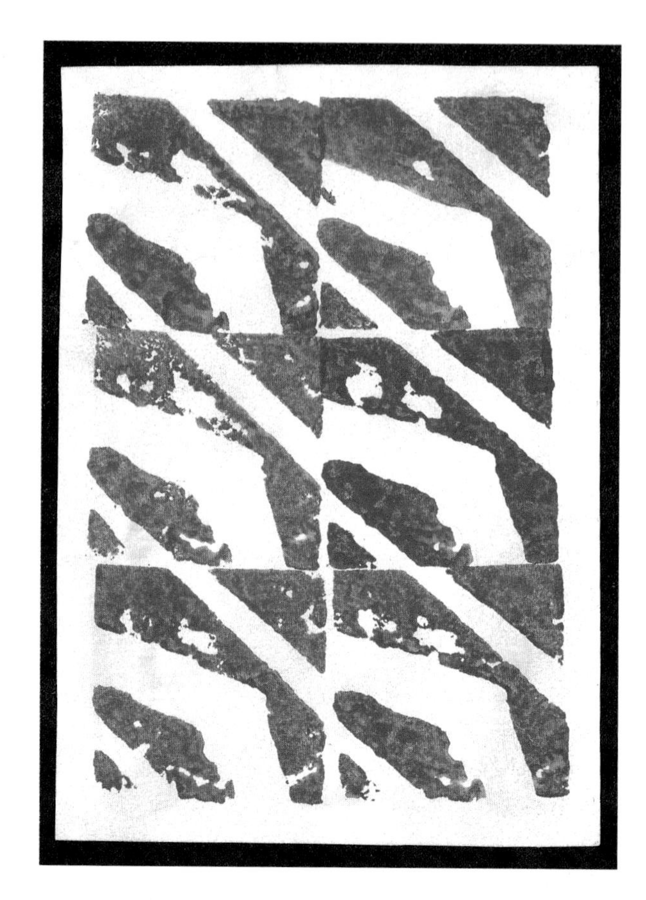

Taking rubbings

You will need:

Thick card, string, PVA glue, glue spreader, brush, scissors, paper, crayons or pencils.

You can take a rubbing from almost any firm textured surface. Make use of things around you: trees, leaves, brickwork, drain lids, tiles, etc. Alternatively, you could make your own surfaces. These can also double up as printing blocks.

Using thick card as a base board, stick down pieces of string or smaller pieces of card. Leave it to dry thoroughly. If you wish to use these blocks for printing as well cover them with a layer of PVA glue. This will seal and strengthen them.

Place the blocks under a piece of paper and using the crayons or pencils, take a rubbing. Remember to use the crayons at an angle and in one direction only for a neat rubbing.

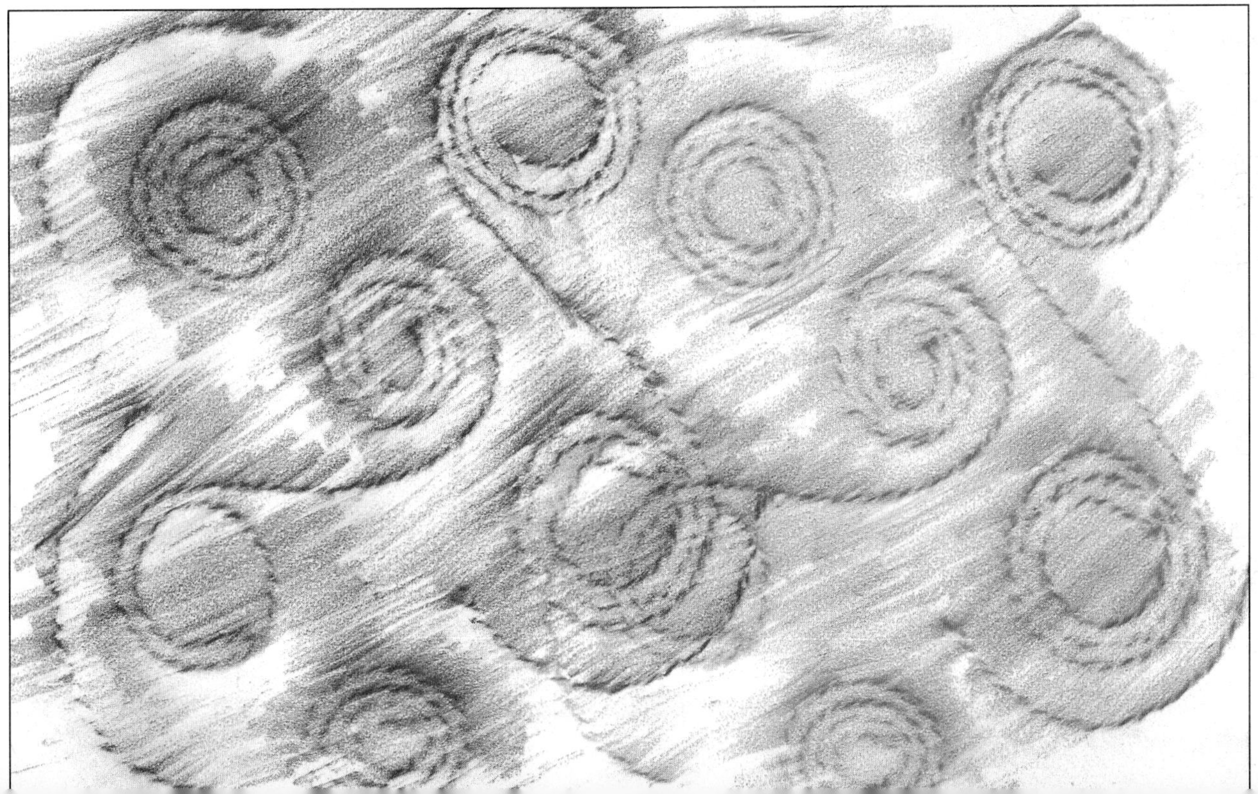

String printing

You will need:

String, paper, paints or inks, saucers or ink trays.

Pour the paint or ink into a saucer and drop in the string so that it is completely covered. Fold your piece of paper in half.

Re-open the paper and place the ink-soaked string on to one half. Make sure that one end of the string goes over the side of the paper. Close the paper again to cover the string. With one hand holding the paper-and-string sandwich firmly closed, use your other hand to pull out the string quickly. Repeat the process using another colour.

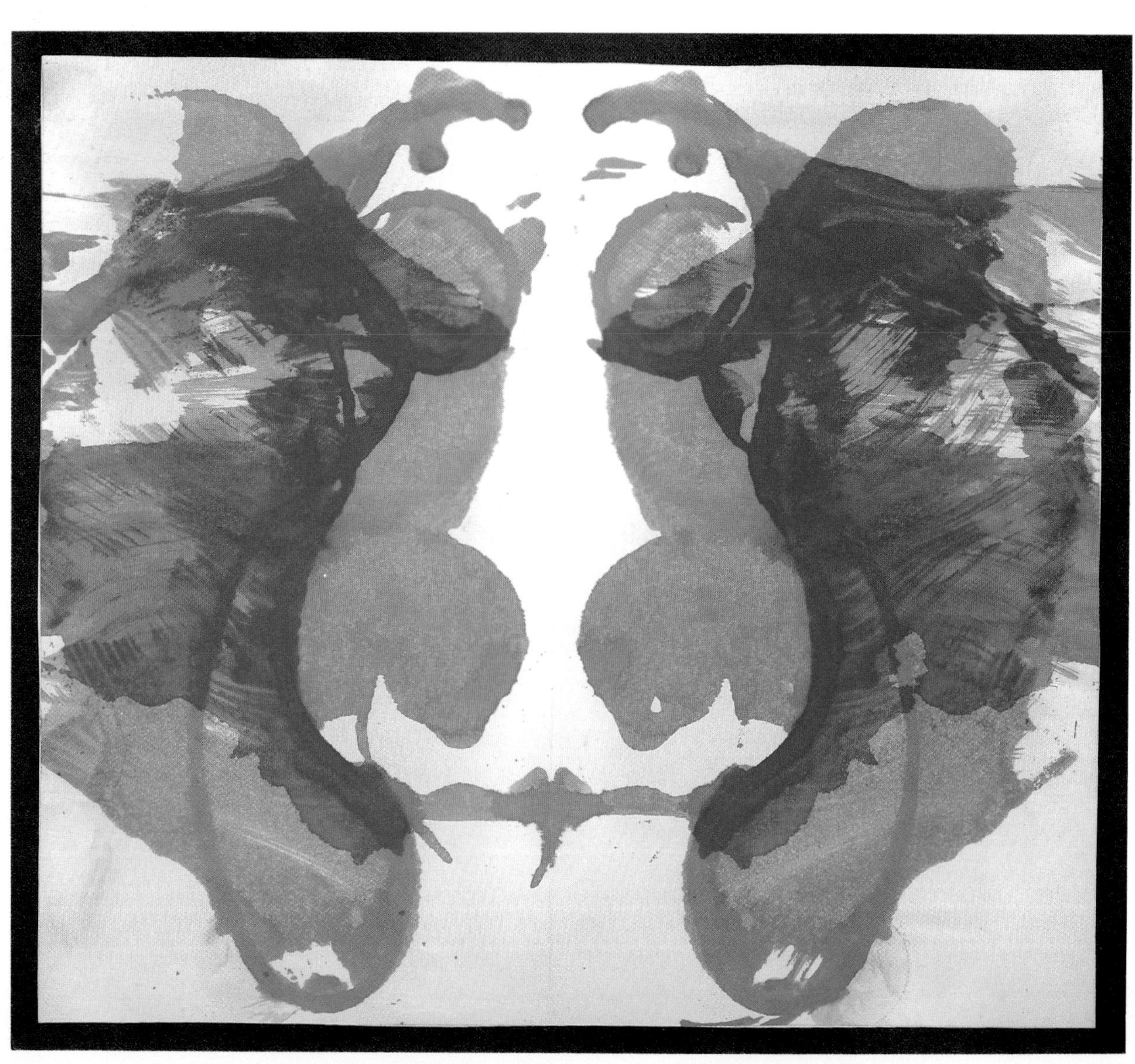

Bubble printing

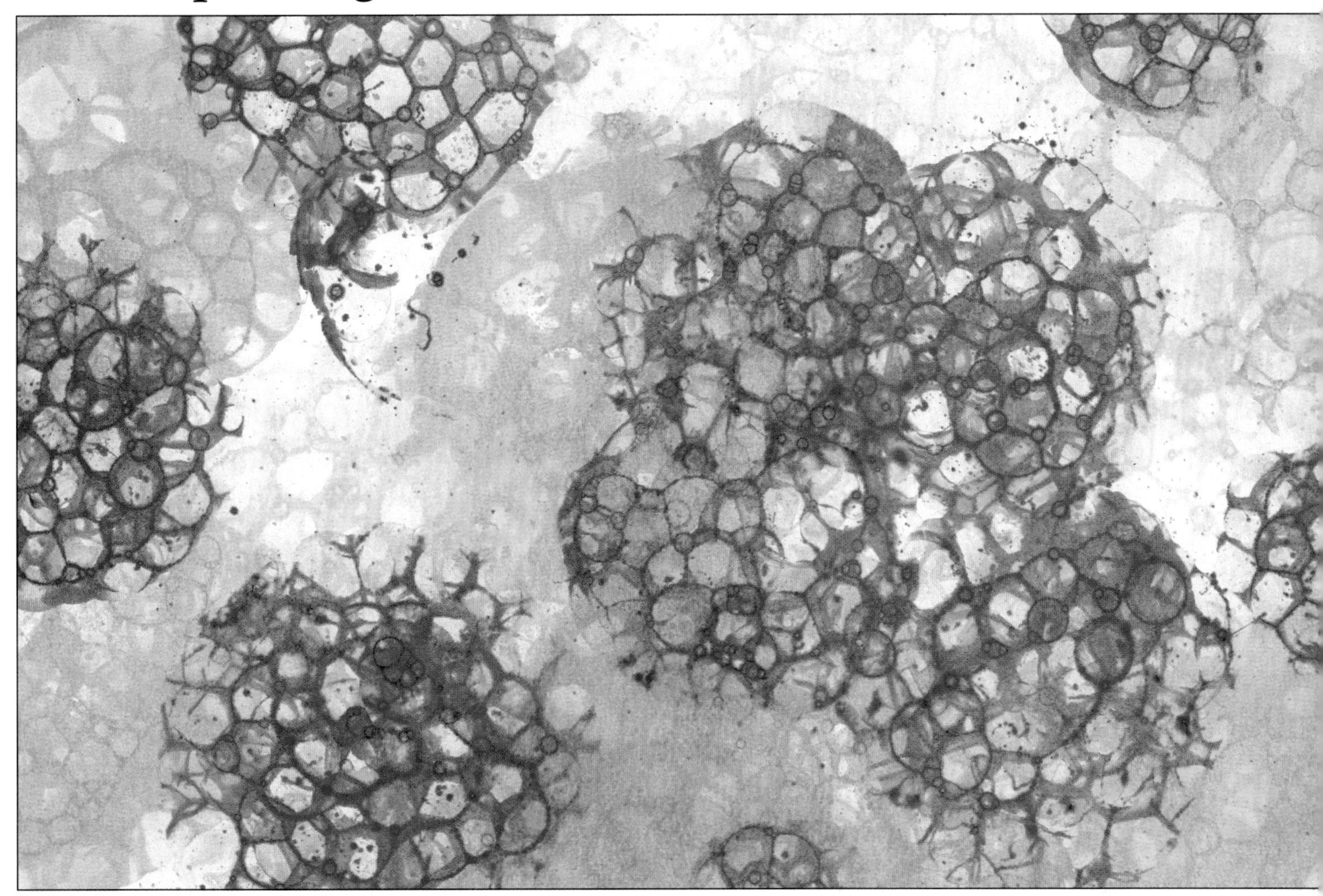

You will need:

Drawing inks, washing-up liquid, straws, paper, small pots with narrow necks.

Drawing inks work best for this activity because they are thin but have a strong pigment. If none are available then thin paints can be used instead. Mix a little washing-up liquid with ink in a small container. Blow through a straw into the mixture until the bubbles froth over the top of the pot. Remove the straw and carefully lay a piece of paper on top of the bubbles to take a print. Repeat using different-coloured inks.

Sponge printing

You will need:

Sponges (preferably the natural ones which have more holes), paints or inks, saucers or ink trays, paper.

Sponges dipped in paint or ink and printed onto paper create a richly textured design. The paints should be fairly thinly mixed and poured into flat containers such as saucers or ink trays. Simply dip the sponges into the paint and print onto a sheet of paper. This is a good technique for covering backgrounds and it is possible to cover a large area quickly.

Monoprinting

You will need:

Ink trays, a perspex sheet or smooth table top, printing inks or paints, paper, scraps of paper, rollers, a pencil.

Monoprinting, as the name suggests, is a method of printing which gives only one print from the original design. Although further prints can be taken, no two prints will be the same. There are two techniques you can use.

Roll some ink onto a smooth surface. Draw a design in the ink with your finger or an old rag. Add more colours if required. Place a sheet of paper over the ink and smooth it down gently with your hand to take a print.

Roll some ink onto a smooth surface. Place a sheet of paper over the ink and use a pencil to draw a design. You must work quickly and avoid pressing onto the paper with your hand. Now peel off the paper to reveal your print. You can then lay a second sheet of paper onto the ink. Press down gently with your hand to take a 'negative' print.

Examples of children's work

This print was made with a polyblock using three colours on black paper. Stephen Holmes, age 6.

This print was made using round objects by Jasmin Wilson, age 5.

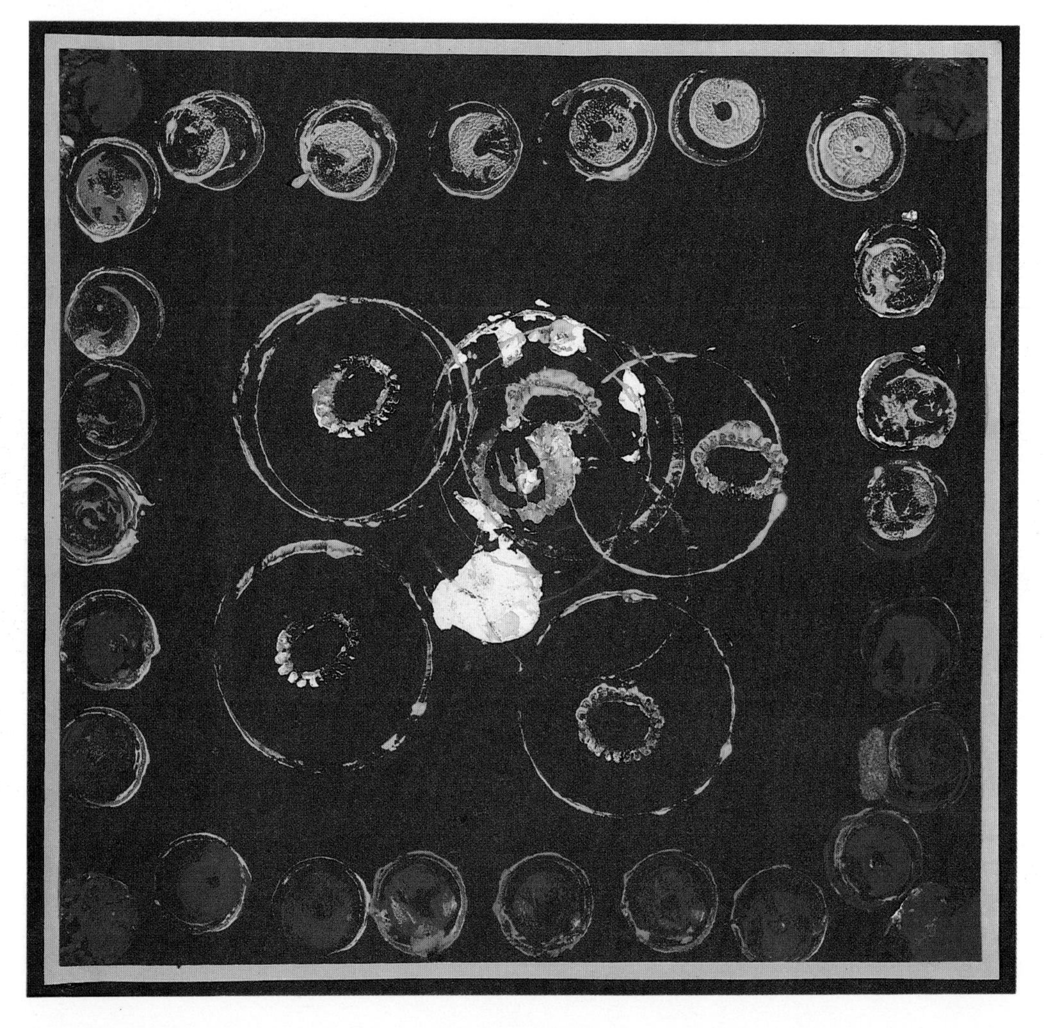

'Spring flowers'. Sponge printing blocks were used by Ben Scoble, age 4.

Potato printing by Hannah Gunn, age 7 (left) and Kerry O'Shea, age 8 (right).

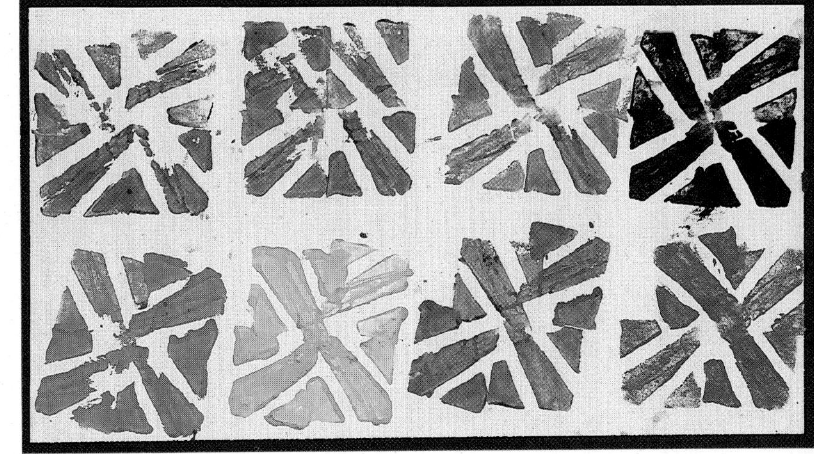

Many teachers have the ability to provide stimulus for artwork by relying on unplanned, unexpected occurrences during the course of the day. Of course, extremely exciting artwork arises from situations like this but not all teachers have the confidence in their ability to seize artistic opportunities. It is sometimes helpful to focus on developing a particular art theme; for example, exploring the qualities of colour, texture or design.

The following activities will give you some ideas to begin developing the theme of 'lines'.

Lines

You will need:

Paper, ruler, pens, crayons, scissors, glue.

Draw vertical lines of varying widths on your paper. This can be done either freehand or can follow precise instructions involving measuring. Then try:

(a) cutting and re-arranging

(b) colouring some lines in and then re-arranging

(c) using regular shapes which can be cut and rotated to change the direction of the lines.

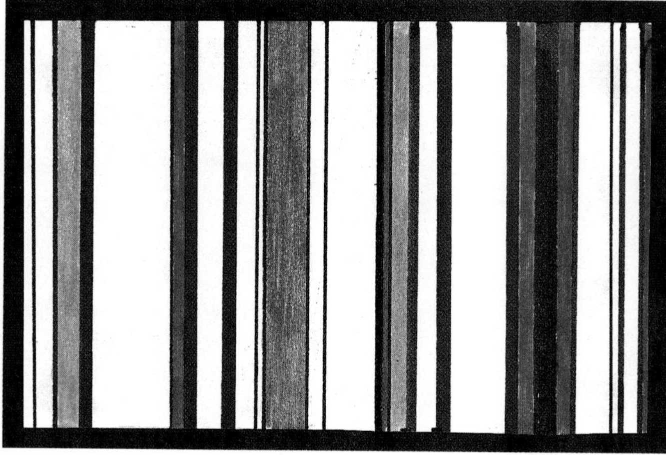

You can then develop this theme by drawing or painting straight lines, putting 'obstacles' in the way to change the direction of the lines.

Experiment with optical effects using straight or wavy lines.

Curve stitching

You will need:

Stiff paper or card, coloured threads, a needle, a ruler.

Begin by drawing two straight lines at right angles to each other in the bottom left-hand corner of your piece of card. Pierce a number of holes, equal distances apart, along each line. (These can be numbered if you wish to make the activity a number operation as well.) Using a needle and thread sew a straight line from the lowest hole on the vertical axis to the farthest hole on the horizontal axis. Your next thread should go from the second hole on the vertical axis to the second farthest hole on the horizontal axis. Continue in this way, moving along a hole each time, until your straight lines create a curve. This principle can also be used with pens or crayons.

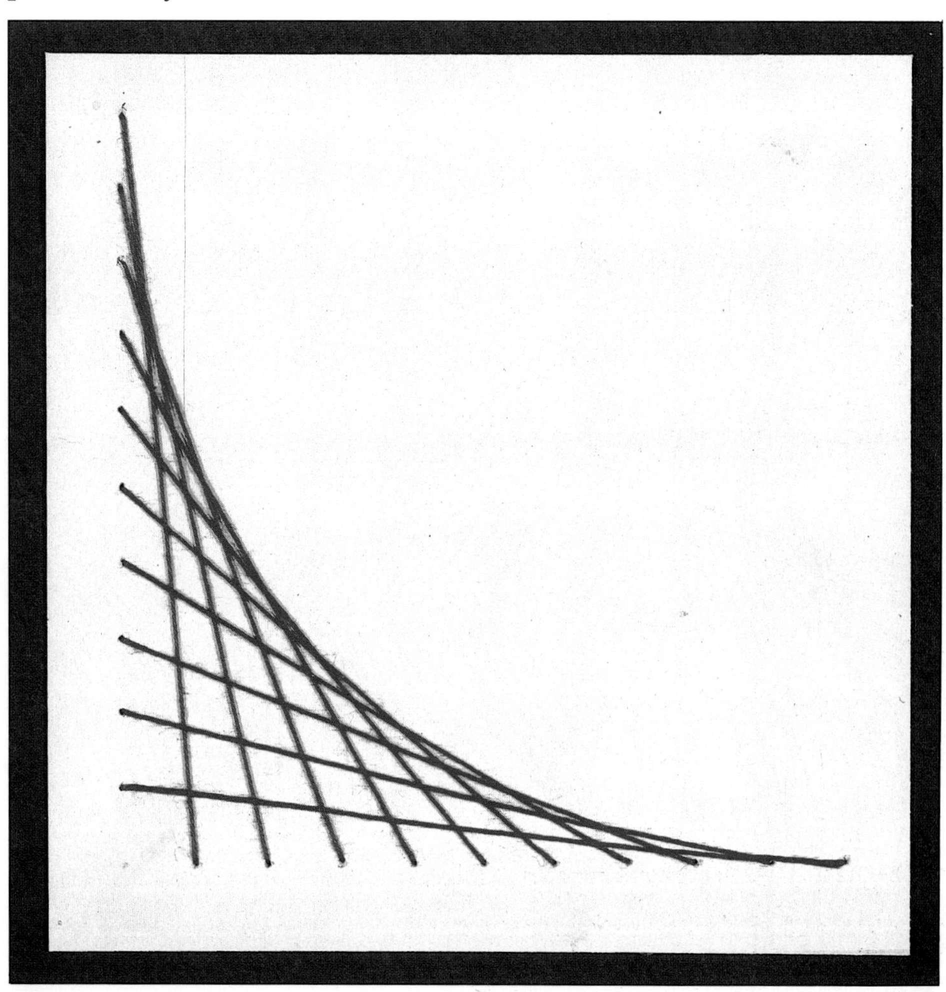

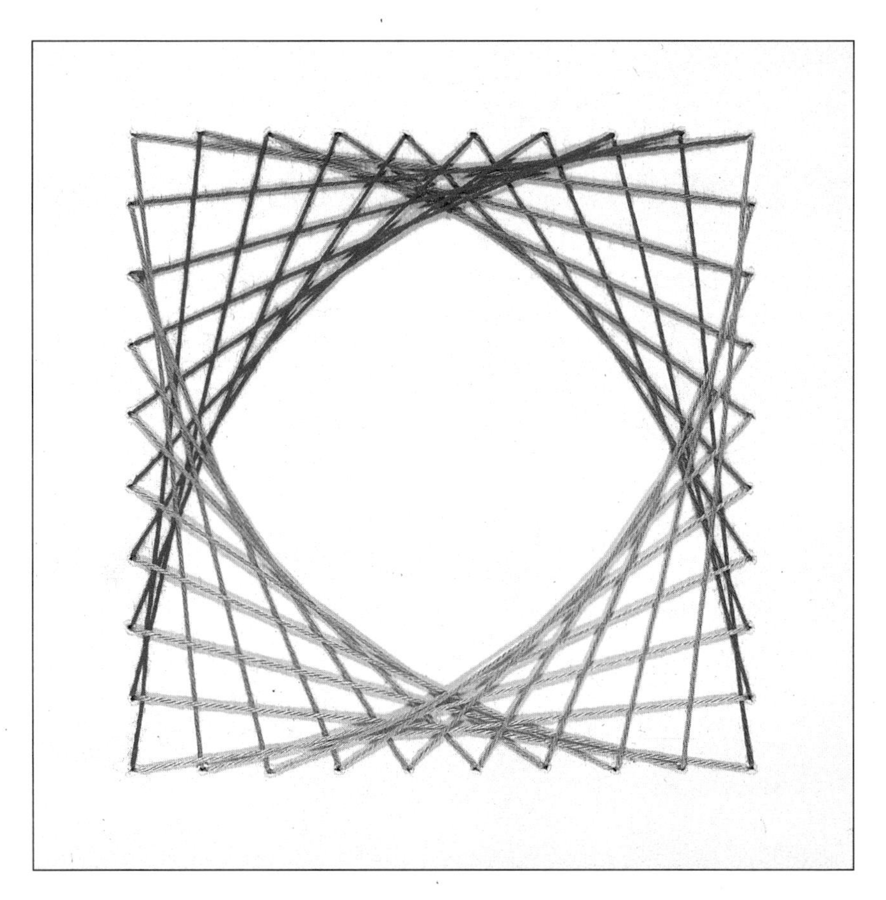

Acknowledgements

Many thanks to the children from Bernwood First School, Botley County Primary School and other friends whose works appear in this book:

Kate Sharkey
Clare Baker
Sam Fitzsimmons
Jack Fitzsimmons
Heather Baker
Nicola Lawson
Isabel Hanson
Natasha Brammer
Paul Bremner
Kevin Rowland
Paul Hart
Hayley Buck
Nicholas Johnson
Lee Butler
Markus Rennie
Robert Sutcliffe
Kirsty Milton
Louisa Matthews
Luke Griffiths
Matthew Drew
Melanie Thurgood
Gillian Colley
Michael Harvey
Stephen Holmes
Jasmin Wilson
Ben Scoble
Hannah Gunn
Kerry O'Shea